YORK FILM NOTES

Fargo

Director
Joel Coen

Note by Susan Levan

Longman   York Press

For Megan and Jack

York Press
322 Old Brompton Road, London SW5 9JH

Pearson Education Limited
Edinburgh Gate, Harlow, Essex CM20 2JE, United Kingdom
Associated companies, branches and representatives throughout
the world

Fargo © 1996 Orion Pictures Corporation. All Rights Reserved.
Stills © 1996 Polygram Filmed Entertainment. All Rights Reserved.
Map by Mike Perkins
Stills supplied by The Kobal Collection
First published 2000

ISBN 0-582-43193-X

Designed by Vicki Pacey
Phototypeset by Gem Graphics, Trenance, Mawgan Porth, Cornwall
Colour reproduction and film output by Spectrum Colour
Printed in Malaysia, KVP

contents

background 5

trailer 5
reading fargo 6
key players' biographies 10
director as auteur 13

narrative & form 19

classical narrative 19
narrative in fargo 21
■ the opening 21
space & time 28
■ space in fargo 29
■ time in fargo 31
character 34
theme as structural device 38
■ the pressure to succeed 39
■ failure to consider others 39
■ the close 39

style 41

signifiers of the real 42
realism 43
signifiers of comedy 43
film blanc? 49
■ film noir stereotypes 49
■ stereotypes in fargo 49
■ visual style of filmnoir 51
■ visual style of fargo 51
■ film noir sound qualities 58
■ sound & style in fargo 58

contexts 61

ideology 61
■ stereotypes 61
■ subversive meaning 63
cultural context 64
■ postmodernism &
post-structuralism 64
■ intertextuality 66
filmography 67
genre 70
■ fargo the western 71
■ fargo the true story 71
■ fargo the thriller 72
■ a comedy western thriller? 72
production history 73
industrial context 76
■ historical background 76
■ independent production 76
audience 78
■ constructing an audience 79
critical responses 82
■ books 82
■ press reviews 83

bibliography 86
cinematic terms 88
credits: fargo 91

AWARDS

Cannes Festival 1996
Best Director: Joel Coen

American Academy Awards (Oscars) 1996
Best Actress: Frances McDormand
Best Original Screenplay: Ethan and Joel Coen

British Academy Awards (Baftas) 1996
David Lean Award for Best Achievement in Direction: Joel Coen

——*//*——

author of this note Susan Levan was born in
December 1946, went to the local grammar school then to college in
Bingley. Qualifying to teach in 1967, she worked in Bradford, London and
Leicestershire before returning to Doncaster, where she teaches at
Doncaster College. She completed her M.A. Film Studies at Sheffield
Hallam University in 2000.

background

trailer *p5*   **reading Fargo** *p6*   **key players' biographies** *p10*
director as auteur *p13*

Fargo, directed by Joel Coen and produced by his brother, Ethan, was released in 1995, the sixth Coen Brothers' movie. Before this film, the Coen brothers had won many fans, but also some critics who found their films too clever and with too little heart. Almost as if in answer to these criticisms they came up with *Fargo*, a celebration of ordinary decent folk. The film won over many of their critics, whilst at the same time pleasing their fans. It tells the story of a kidnapping gone wrong and a pregnant policewoman who, without any loss of composure, brings the criminals to justice. Marking something of a change of style for the brothers, it is less whimsical and rather more self-effacing than their previous films, though there remains a subtle but distinctive humour.

trailer

The Coen brothers have created a wonderful contemporary folk legend – a Winter's Tale with a haunting, melancholy score, a beautiful, grave look and a magisterial, fatalistic rhythm.

Will Cohu, Sunday Express, 2 June 1996, p. 59

... an eye-poppingly weird and wonderful black comedy movie ...

US Daily Mail, 8 December 1995, p. 42

Okay, *Fargo* is better than 98% of what's out there.

Georgia Brown, Village Voice, 12 March 1996, p. 46

Managing to persuade us that the pregnant woman's face is more interesting to contemplate than hoodlums pumping lead into each other might just be *Fargo*'s – and the Coen brothers' most audacious achievement.

Jonathon Coe, New Statesman and Society, 7 June 1996, p. 6

Nothing, of course, shows up blood the way snow does, and there is plenty of both.

Philip French, Observer Review, 2 June 1996, p. 10

No previous film from the Coen brothers has contained such human characters.

Times, 30 May 1996, p. 37

Why let truth get in the way of a good story.

Karen Steen, Guardian, The Guide, 11–17 October 1997, p. 121

I can't help but wonder if perhaps this whole spiel about *Fargo* being based on a true incident might be a tale of some height.

Chris Peachment, Sunday Telegraph Review, 26 May 1996, p. 8

And Steve Buscemi, [who] has now taken over from James Woods as the actor most likely to be cast as a rat-faced sleazeball is a disreputable joy.

Kevin Jackson, The Independent on Sunday, 2 June 1996

We're laughing at the Coen's smartness and cynicism – at a virtuoso piece of writing, rather than an organic piece of drama.

Quentin Curtis, Daily Telegraph, 31 May 1996, p. 22

Fargo, directed by Joel Coen and written by Coen and his brother, Ethan, is a subtle, beautifully photographed thriller.

William Leith, Mail on Sunday, 2 June 1996, p. 31

Fargo is a crime film with character.

Alexander Walker, Evening Standard, 30 May 1996, pp. 26–27

Fargo is a complex thriller and a compelling hit.

Steve Wright, The Sun, 31 May 1996, p. 17

reading fargo

Fargo was written by Ethan and Joel Coen, directed by Joel and produced by Ethan. At least that is what appears on the credits, though in interviews the two brothers hold that they co-operate on everything (see Director as Auteur). As the film begins, a caption tells us that it is based on a true story, but we are also told that the events are fictional and characters are not intended to resemble any real person. Why the contradiction? The plot involves that darkest of crimes, very bloody murder, yet the screen is frequently white and there lurks – in the flat white landscape and the apparent banality of everyday life – not only murder, but humour.

The story tells of a car salesman, Jerry Lundegaard, in Minneapolis who, having serious financial problems, decides to hire two low-life characters to kidnap his wife, Jean. The plan is that Jerry's father-in-law, Wade

Gustafson – who is also his boss – should give Jerry money to pay the ransom on his daughter's life. Jerry would then pay off the two kidnappers and pocket a sizeable chunk of the ransom himself. Needless to say, it does not quite work like that. Jerry is blessed with very little foresight or judgement, Wade is not given to handing money over to a son-in-law whom he considers incompetent, and the two kidnappers have little rapport, still less patience and no morality whatsoever. They do, however, have guns, axes and a car. Soon they are driving around Minnesota leaving multiple corpses and a trail of blood in the snow. This, naturally, is where the cops come in. Chief Marge Gunderson, seven months pregnant and a very nice woman married to a very nice man, hauls her ungainly body around the screen, politely and pleasantly questioning witnesses and making astute and accurate assessments of the situation. Eventually she discovers all and without so much as a hint of a hesitation, she does what a pregnant cop has to do. As the kidnappers inevitably turn on each other, she resolutely captures the remaining villain and takes him in, expressing her sadness at his crimes, and returns home to her husband, Norm.

In keeping with what we might expect of a Coen brothers' film, the humour is quirky and low-key rather than broad or hilarious. Much of it arises from character and from the incongruity of the individuals with their situations. How can a seven months pregnant woman deal with serial killers? What makes poor ineffectual Jerry think he can handle the underworld, even outwit it, when he can barely handle his son, his customers, or his father-in-law? How can these homely Midwestern folk, with their singsong local accent influenced by Scandinavian ancestry, their polite and unexcitable manners, snow-trudging gait and ultraordinariness, possibly be involved in such a bloodbath? 'It's a real shame', says Marge, looking at the first victim, a state trooper. The most ordinary (one might even say boring) of diners, hotels, car parks, kitchens, offices and car showrooms provide the surroundings for a story of violence and death. Even the roads are flat and straight, but we have seen that before in Coen movies (see Director as Auteur). These brothers were raised in Minnesota and the fact that they portray its inhabitants as ordinary is possibly a mark of familiarity. One thing is certain, they have gone out of their way to represent the good people of Minnesota as bland, unemotional and almost inscrutable. So it is with great subtlety that the actors who play them have invested their roles with the right emotional tones, since finding the balance somewhere between complete sang-froid and too much visible emotion must have required considerable observation and understanding, as well as a script which creates just the right dialogue and conditions.

THE CHARACTERS

Jerry Lundegaard (played by William H. Macey) is seen from the very first scene as a man who cannot win. Here, as he goes immediately on the defensive after being accused of being late, his face has the look of a somewhat crumpled little Pinnocchio, or the uptight dummy of some sadistic ventriloquist. His eyes have gone past the point of anxiety and reached that glazed look of long-term suffering. We suffer for Jerry. We squirm with embarrassment. He stammers his way through conversations with people who always hold him in contempt, from his father-in-law to those to whom he tries to sell cars with TruCoat under-seal. When Marge Gunderson treats him with brisk and pleasant courtesy, he appears stunned, speechless, a rabbit in the headlights of her innocent gaze. With each new twist to his plan, we know that he is digging deeper holes for himself. Yet although we can sense his desperation, seldom does Jerry show overt emotion. He once takes out his frustration on the icy windscreen of his car, and once on the office phone and desk, but never when in the company of others. At the end of the film, however, he is a sobbing wreck, still trying to wriggle free.

Marge Gunderson (played by Frances McDormand) is no more given to displays of emotion than Jerry. You might say that her chief, long-term emotion is placid contentment. Marge is incorruptible because she does not desire the things that she does not have. She and her nice husband, Norm (John Carroll Lynch) – like the *Tellytubbies* on children's television – love each other very much, but with big meals rather than big hugs. They eat together, a great deal and often. She buys worms for his fishing trips and hands them over as the two of them eat; he gets eggs for her breakfast and burgers for her office lunch. They wait for the birth of their baby. Norm works from home, painting wildlife pictures for postage stamps whilst his wife has the active career outside the home. Marge Gunderson is surely a country cousin of Mary Beth Lacey of the popular American television series of the Eighties, *Cagney and Lacey*. Lacey was the home-loving partner in a female cop duo who liked to get back to her husband, Harve, and who was frequently seen settling down for the night in bed with him. She, too had a pregnancy featured in the series, and was astute, hard-working and incorruptible. *Fargo* shows Marge and Norm at home in bed, sometimes watching TV, with Marge usually wearing a cardigan to keep warm and cosy. Their relationship is one of comfort.

Of the two hired kidnapper/murderers, one, Carl Showalter (Steve Buscemi), is small, bad-tempered, mobile and loquacious. He seeks out the company of hookers and is in general gregarious and volatile. He constantly is described as 'kinda funny lookin'. On the other hand his partner, Gaear Grimsrud (Peter Stormare), is big, blond and nearly silent. It is the latter of the pair who is first to kill. He is cold-blooded and taciturn and kills for convenience as most people swat annoying flies. Carl kills for money and in temper. One of the broadest jokes in the film is given to Carl who, after being wounded in the jaw by Wade's bullet, returns with his spoils to Gaear, holding a bloodstained paper to his jaw. Bursting into the cabin hideout, Carl says as Gaear turns to look at him, 'You should she zhe ozher guy!' (spelling as in the Coen's screenplay).

The comedy, then, resides largely with the characters, all of whom are subtly played, and with a script which ensures that every character has his or her moments. Additionally, the accent of Minnesota affords great amusement. Never can a film have made such frequent and varied use of the word 'Yah', inflected as a question, an answer, a reassurance, an encouragement. Phrases like 'Okey-dokey, thanks a bunch', 'Heck' and 'Aw, geez', are apparently in common use out there. The sound design offers splashing blood, jingling bells and the sickening noise approximating to what the pushing of a body through a wood chipper might possibly sound like. The specially written music, an arrangement of a Scandinavian folk tune and hymn, is strong and memorable with the rhythm of a slow, ponderous dance. And then there are the visual jokes, a socked foot sticking out of the wood chipper which is one of the film's most memorable images and Norm's worms on the table beside the burgers. The bleak, frozen white of the outdoors with no horizon, deserted open spaces and car parks, breath on cold air, woolly gloves and bulky clothing all give the film a distinctive visual style.

All in all it seems that the Coens might have decided not to turn this crime story into film noir (see Style: Stereotypes Associated with Film Noir), with its shadowy expressionism, night scenes and paranoid characters in a claustrophobic city of murder, suspense and deceit. Instead they have used bright, white, snowy light and many daytime scenes. There are comfortable, bland, homely people in a wide open, rural setting where violent crime is seldom seen, where there is little suspense as the viewer knows what is happening and can usually see what is going to happen, and where the *femme* is definitely not *fatale*. The Coens have given us murder on a Christmas card. One might say they had deliberately invented film blanc!

key players' biographies

These biographies of key players are not comprehensive, but examples of work have been selected as being representative of the actors' background and experience which made them suitable for casting in *Fargo*.

FRANCES MCDORMAND (MARGE)

Frances McDormand studied at the Yale School of Drama and is married to Joel Coen. She has worked in the theatre, including on Broadway where she has played Stella, the plain wife of brutish Stanley Kowalski and sister of Blanche du Bois in Tennessee Williams's *A Streetcar Named Desire*. On television she was a regular in the *Hill Street Blues* cop series and she has appeared in television movies. For the cinema she has made more than fifteen films. Although her role as Marge in *Fargo* requires a subtle appreciation of the comic, McDormand has played straight or serious roles equally well. For example she played a policeman's wife who informs the FBI of the murderous Ku Klux Klan activities of her husband and his friends, and is roundly beaten for having done so, in Alan Parker's *Mississippi Burning* (1988). She has also appeared in left-wing British director, Ken Loach's film about Northern Ireland, *Hidden Agenda* which won the Jury Prize at the Cannes Festival in 1990. With her pleasant, non-glamorous image, McDormand has been cast in some out of the ordinary parts requiring an intelligent approach and understanding. She was in *Blood Simple* and *Raising Arizona*, also Coen brothers' films.

WILLIAM H. MACY (JERRY)

William H. Macy is considered a character actor, that is he tends to play rather eccentric roles. He is credited on many feature films: Woody Allen's *Radio Days* (1987) and his *Shadows and Fog* (1991), Jeremiah Chechik's *Benny and Joon* (1993), Stephen Herek's *Mr Holland's Opus* (1995), Peter Yates's *Roommates* (also in 1995), and David S. Ward's *Down Periscope* (1996). Macy has also appeared in four David Mamet films: *House of Games*, Mamet's directorial debut in 1987, *Things Change* (1988), *Homicide* (1991) on which Macy worked with Roger Deakins, the same cinematographer as on *Fargo*; and *Oleanna* (1994). In television, Macy plays Dr Morganstern in the popular series *ER* and has appeared in *LA Law* and several other series, mini-series and television movies less well-known in Britain than in America. His stage credits include the Broadway production of *Our Town* which won a Tony Award, and many off-Broadway productions such as a stage version of Mamet's *Oleanna* for which he was nominated Best Actor for the Outer Critics Circle Award. In addition to his acting career, William H. Macy has directed several plays in the theatre and *Oleanna* in a Los Angeles production. He has written several scripts including an episode of *Thirty Something*.

STEVE BUSCEMI (CARL)

Steve Buscemi took up drama in his senior year of high school. He then studied with John Strasberg in Manhattan. He worked with the Coen brothers on three films before *Fargo*: *Miller's Crossing* (1990), *Barton Fink* (1991) and *The Hudsucker Proxy* (1994). He also played the role of Donny in *The Big Lebowski* (1998). He has made over forty-five films since 1985, some of the best known (apart from the Coen brothers' films) being Jim Jarmusch's *Mystery Train* (1989), Robert Benton's *Billy Bathgate* (1991) which was written by Tom Stoppard from a Doctorow gangster novel; Quentin Tarantino's *Reservoir Dogs* (1992) and *Pulp Fiction* (1994); Robert Rodriguez's *Desperado* (1995); Tom DiCillio's Sundance Film Festival Award winning independent film *Living in Oblivion* (1995); Gary Fleder's *Things to*

Do in Denver When You're Dead (1995), and Stanley Tucci and Campbell Scott's *Big Night* (1996). Steve Buscemi won a Spirit Award for his role as Mr Pink in *Reservoir Dogs* and a Spirit Award nomination for *Mystery Train*. Even this short selection from his work is a demonstration of Buscemi's association with independent, even alternative film. Indeed *Living in Oblivion* is an independent film which is actually about independent film making. Steve Buscemi also is moving into writing and directing. He wrote, directed and acted in a short film called *What Happened to Pete* (1992) for a cable network in America and has completed his first feature film, *Trees Lounge* (1996). He is something of a star in the offbeat, independent film world (see Contexts).

HARVE PRESNELL (WADE)

Harve Presnell returned to film in 1996 after an absence of twenty-five years. He is perhaps best known for his roles in Joshua Logan's *Paint Your Wagon* (1969) and Charles Walters's *The Unsinkable Molly Brown* (1964), both musical-comedies. He has played Daddy Warbucks in *Annie* on Broadway and he was first to play Rhett Butler in the musical version of *Gone with the Wind* in London. He has recorded a performance in *Carmina Burana* with Eugene Ormandy and the Philadelphia Symphony Orchestra. The rich quality of his voice and the association with confident, mature male roles makes him ideal for intimidating the stammering Jerry in *Fargo*.

PETER STORMARE (GAEAR)

Peter Stormare has, among other things, appeared in Ingmar Bergman's *Fanny and Alexander* (1982), Penny Marshall's *Awakenings* (1990), and Louis Malle's *Damage* (1992). He has also frequently acted for the National Theatre of Sweden, sometimes with Bergman, for example on *Miss Julie* and *King Lear*. He has written and directed for the National Theatre of Sweden, and in New York, Tokyo and London. He has worked, too, in Swedish television and radio. In short he is probably the epitome of Swedishness for anyone casting Swedish roles. He played a German nihilist in *The Big Lebowski* (1998).

JOHN CARROLL LYNCH (NORM)

John Carroll Lynch went to the Catholic University of America in Washington DC. He has worked in the theatre in his native Colorado and for eight years in Minneapolis. In film he has appeared in Donald Petrie's *Grumpy Old Men* (1993), Peter Horton's *The Cure* (1995), Steven Baigelman's *Feeling Minnesota* (1996), and Ted Demme's *Beautiful Girls* (1996). Also he has worked in television.

KRISTIN RUDRUD (JEAN)

Kristin Rudrud is a graduate of Moorhead State University and also attended the London Academy of Music and Dramatic Art. She has played Jessica in *A Merchant of Venice* and Celimene in *The Misanthrope*, Katherine in *Amadeus* and Peaseblossom in *A Midsummer Night's Dream*. Film works include Alan Rudolph's *Equinox* (1992). She has appeared in American television's *All My Children*.

director as auteur

Originally, the term auteur, used by French film critics, referred to a film maker who was both writer and director of a film. Literally translated, it simply means author. The term was used as long ago as the Twenties to refer to writer-directors of silent films who were considered a cut above mere directors who did only the mise-en-scène of material written by someone else. An auteur had something of the status of artist or creator, as opposed to that of a craftsperson.

In an art form which involves many people (as credit lists show), there has been constant debate about how much meaning can be ascribed to the film's director alone.

In the academic world, the advent of cultural studies during the Seventies placed film firmly in its wider context, ensuring that a director (whether or not afforded the title of auteur) could be seen merely as one of many interacting factors producing meaning in a film. The phases through which auteur 'theory' (for want of a better term) has gone are summarised as follows:

phases of auteur theory

- 1920s: The term auteur was used in France to refer to a film maker who both wrote and directed his or her own films. Under these terms, Joel Coen would have qualified as an auteur
- 1950s: The *Cahiers* group saw the director as central, as the sole producer of meaning in a film. Understanding a film was bound up with understanding its auteur, but application of the term was extended to include those who may not actually have written their own films, but had a distinctive, recognisable style. This description could be applied to Coen
- 1960s: Structuralism introduced other influences on the production of meaning in film: the 'language' and grammatical conventions of film, the ways in which film-making institutions work, social contexts and technology were all seen by critics and theorists as structures making a film's meaning. Coen, as director of films, would be one of the many meaning makers
- 1970s: Post-structuralism introduced notions of ideology; a film text began to be seen not only as carrying the meanings put into it by those individuals and institutions who made it, but also as being in a relationship with those watching it. The meaning in film is seen here as affected by the standpoint of the audience, by psychological readings, readings from different political perspectives, and by the film's relationship not only with its director and its audience, but with other texts (intertextuality)

Any film or media studies text book will have a section on authorship or auteur theory with advice on further reading (see Bibliography).

JOEL AND ETHAN COEN, AUTEURS

The Coens are the sons of teachers and were brought up in Minnesota. Joel, born in 1955, is the elder and studied Film at New York University's film school, whilst his younger brother, Ethan, born in 1958, studied Philosophy.

Immediately we consider Joel Coen as an auteur we must start to answer questions. Are his films Joel Coen films or are they Coen brothers' films? It has to be said that generally the two brothers are considered together as the films' auteurs. They are interviewed together for the purposes of promoting their films on television and in magazines. Here is an instant departure from convention which says that a film is referred to as e.g. a Martin Scorsese film or a Jim Jarmusch film. In an interview, a director may be asked to discuss the fact that she or he frequently works with a particular writer or producer, but in the case of the Coens, the two brothers seem to be treated as co-auteurs of their films. They claim that they write, direct and produce together, that they merely appear on the credits as having specific titles. So we are dealing with films which may be said to be the works of at least two creative talents. For our purposes here, Joel and Ethan Coen together are taken to be the auteurs of *Fargo*.

Today, probably most people would consider it naïve to assume that the full understanding of any film is simply a question of understanding its director's intentions. Certainly with Coen brothers' movies, our appreciation is increased by not only some acquaintance with the sense of humour of the pair, but also by an understanding of the system within which they make their films, and most certainly by a knowledge of the history of the genres in which they work. The relationship of *Fargo* to other thrillers (if thriller is what it is) is dealt with later, as are its mode of production and some of the critical responses (see Contexts). What we can look at here is what might be understood by the term 'a Coen brothers' film', i.e. some of the hallmarks.

Fargo, released in 1996, is the sixth film written, directed and produced by the Coen brothers and released since 1984. *Blood Simple* (1984), *Raising Arizona* (1987), *Miller's Crossing* (1989), *Barton Fink* (1991), *The Hudsucker Proxy* (1994) and *The Big Lebowski* (1998) are also amongst the Coens' body of work. The movies often relate in some way to one or more of the popular genres (see Contexts: Filmography and Genre).

The Coens' use of genre has the effect of setting up expectations and then swiping the mat from under our feet, so that we are forced to look anew at both what we had been expecting and what we have got. It has the effect of deconstructing constructs which we had taken for granted and alerts us both to what those old expectations were and to what the Coens are putting in their place. Deconstruction is a concept associated with postmodern, post-structuralist (see Contexts) counter cinema which very deliberately sets out not to be like established cinemas, but in doing so, often demonstrates considerable understanding of the cinema it opposes in both its practices and values. This can certainly be said of the films of Joel and Ethan Coen; they are genre films of a new generation, and like many a new generation they are both a product of the old and to some extent a rebellion against it.

Coen films play with notions of genre, use crimes gone wrong as starting points, and have very complex stories in which every character is so busy pursuing his or her own ends that the actions, thoughts and feelings of others are not seen. Almost like the Whitehall farces once so popular in English theatres, the characters try to extricate themselves from one mess after another without ever reflecting on the consequences, or stopping to try to work out what the other characters might do next. But the Coens' films have a very dark side, too. The initial crime is often the result of someone trying to achieve the perfect life by taking what they lack away from someone else. The pressure to have that perfect life is seen as a motivation for crime. Hi and Ed in *Raising Arizona* steal a baby when they cannot have one of their own. Jerry in *Fargo* invents ways of becoming what he feels his wife and father-in-law think he should be, rich and successful. There is a tendency for rich, often older or powerful men to be unsympathetic, domineering characters with negative effects on those around them, manipulating, exploiting and despising those who are weaker or poorer than themselves. Each of the films has such a character.

Some images in the films can be read as metaphor. A long, flat, straight road is often used as a location for deeds which are anything but on the straight and narrow. The straight road leading from one place to another, shot from a low angle to emphasise surface and perspective, ironically and metaphorically indicates that nobody knows where the deeds done will end. *Blood Simple, Raising Arizona, Fargo* and *The Big Lebowski* all make use of a version of this road shot. From a similar low angle, Tom Reagan's hat is seen blowing away along a woodland ride in *Miller's Crossing*. In the title sequence at the start of *Fargo*, there is a white frame into which car headlights slowly appear as reference points, revealing the white to be snow and the scene to be a road, straight but sometimes undulating. This sets the scene for a story in which the metaphorical road and the horizon between right and wrong are for many characters as blurred as the road and the horizon in the title sequence. Visibility is poor, both literally and metaphorically, and life has ups and downs.

Repetitions of lines of dialogue and similar shots can be seen to emphasise similarities and differences between characters. *Fargo* has two informants who describe Carl as 'funny looking' so we know they mean the same man. Jerry and Marge share the same singsong dialect and pointedly use similar phrases, creating irony in the dissimilarity of their characters. Several characters watch television: Marge and Norm in bed, Jean Lundegaard just before being kidnapped, while later Jean's killer, Gaear Grimsrud watches melodrama in close proximity to her dead body. Marge and Norm sit at tables together and this emphasises the humdrum routine of their existence. But when Marge sits at a table with an estranged old school friend, the similarity emphasises the opposite, the lack of that humdrum intimacy.

Arguably most poignant of all, each of the films has humour. This is possibly what fans of these films like most. It is the kind of humour usually described as quirky (having little oddities or idiosyncrasies), wry (skewed or lopsided) and ironic (perverse, seeming to say one thing but in fact meaning the opposite, or delivered at the best time for humour but the worst for the characters). It is perhaps one of the most difficult of tasks to describe humour, and even doing so well does not guarantee that someone else will find a humour funny. Some do not find Coen humour funny, they even find it offensive. However, it is not a condescending humour. It assumes a measure of knowledge and understanding on the part of the audience, who have to know something of Hollywood film's history in order to see what the Coens are saying, and to find it amusing. It is not broad or zany and it does not explain itself. But it has been said of the Coen brothers that they are not trying to be liked by everyone (see Peter Korte's *'Interview: "We don't want everybody to love us"'* in *Joel and Ethan Coen*, p. 7, Peter Korte and Georg Seesslen (eds)). Their jokes are esoteric, for those in the know. The Coen brothers claim to do what they do for fun, because they find it amusing, not to cater for majority taste.

Although the Coens do not always use the same crew nor, of course the same actors, there are people in both cast and crew who have worked on more than one of their films. Carter Burwell has done the music in all seven Coen films. Frances McDormand has appeared in three and the part of Marge Gunderson was written with her in mind. Steve Buscemi has worked with the Coens five times. Cinematographer Roger Deakins (who is British) has made four films with the Coens: *Barton Fink, The Hudsucker Proxy, Fargo* and *The Big Lebowski. Fargo* is the second of three Coen films to be produced by Working Title Films. There is to some extent a repertory feel to the Coens' working methods, since they often seem to like to join up with people they have worked with before, making a sort of extended company of collaborators.

The term postmodern is often used to describe the work of the Coen brothers. This is a term which has no easy definition. Their telling of stories which comment on the nature of stories and of storytelling, their reaction against classic genres, their turning over and examination of genre stereotypes and conventions from within their films, are all part of what is being referred to when they are said to be postmodern. The word refers both to the time at which the films were made and to the films' meanings (see Contexts). On the subject, the Coen brothers themselves would doubtless be content with not addressing questions of meaning and postmodernity. They would say that, like Norville Barnes's hula hoops in *The Hudsucker Proxy*, their work is just for fun, for kids.

narrative & form

classical narratives *p19*   the narrative in Fargo *p21*   space & time *p28*
characters *p34*   theme as structural device *p38*

When we watch a film, we are picking up clues and reading messages all the time. Possibly we have expectations and have seen the film's certificate from a board which classifies films. If watching on television, we are aware of the time of day at which it is put out. We may have already seen films from the same director or of the same genre. Indeed, it is probably our expectations which led us to watch the film in the first place. We watch expectantly. The film's writer and director have planned and executed a route for us through those linked events we call the story. A plot is slowly unfolding.

The Coen brothers have made their movies in a time when there have been many challenges to 'classical' narration. Film directors now often study film in a university. As a film student himself, Joel Coen has had his attention drawn to questions of narrative and the numerous alternatives to classical Hollywood style which exist. His postmodern era is a very knowing, not a very innocent one. However, after making several films of a somewhat 'flashier' narrative style than those of classic Hollywood's, he has chosen to return to a more classical style in *Fargo*.

In the light of a little understanding of the old Hollywood style, and using some of the language attached to the study of narrative, the organisation and telling of the story of *Fargo* can be examined. It always helps in understanding matters of narration, to bear in mind that films are constructed from carefully considered, individual shots, thoughtfully joined together and then dubbed with specially designed sound. Films are not filmed plays.

classical narrative

There is a period in the history of Hollywood which is often referred to as 'classical'. This period, which begins with narrative (storytelling) film during the silent era, is in place before 1920, and ends by 1960. Classical narrative style is easy for the viewer to watch and understand. Everything about it is geared to passing on required information to the viewer. The narrative of *Fargo* is reminiscent of this style, whose characteristics are that the beginnings of stories are often seen as disruptions to everyday life, usually occurring early in the film, which clearly-defined characters are then motivated to resolve. The disruption of normality is the starting point. The characters who must resolve the disruption and the forces which oppose them lead the action in a cause-effect drama, ending – usually after a crisis point – in resolution where a new normality is achieved. We can see Jerry as the protagonist whose life is disrupted, and whose quest is opposed, but he departs from the classical idea of a protagonist in that he is not clearly either good or bad and is opposed by forces of both good and evil.

Each event in the story is seen as the result of a previous event. There is a causal link between events which is not always present in real life. The viewer is orientated as a spectator almost as if watching always from one side of the room or set. In Hollywood there grew to be conventions about editing, so that an ordinary cut from one shot to the next kept continuity and could be made very smooth by e.g. matches on action and eye-line matches. Also needed for continuity is keeping the viewer's focal point in the same part of the screen across cuts (very important on the big screen where a change of focal point on screen can mean a turn of the head for viewers) and, in short, making the audience as unaware of cuts as possible, so that they almost enter into the film's world. We can summarise these basics in the following points:

■ stories of disruption, quest and resolution

■ clearly-defined characters whose motivation moves the story along

■ cause and effect links between events

■ continuity editing

The whole point of such narrative style was to not to draw attention to itself, but to draw people into the story. The term 'classical' is probably that given to narratives like this by David Bordwell (see Bibliography).

narrative in fargo

Events in *Fargo* are revealed in chronological order. There are no flashes back or forth. The audience has an omniscient view of events and sees more than any one of the characters. Nothing except some of the music occurs outside the diegesis and the narrative style is unobtrusive, quietly functional and self-effacing.

THE OPENING

The title sequence comes before the first scene of the action of the film. This is, of course, designed to reveal something about the film. After the distributor's name has faded from the black background, a caption fades in over the black, as the solemn theme music begins very quietly. It reads:

```
This is a true story. The events depicted in
this film took place in Minnesota in 1987. At
the request of the survivors, the names have
been changed. Out of respect for the dead, the
rest has been told exactly as it occurred
```

This can be compared with the declaration after the end of the film and after the credits, that all characters and all events are entirely fictional and no similarity to any real person alive or dead is intended. It may be joke number one! Nevertheless the caption sets in place the underlying association with documentary and realism. Tricks with time would seem inappropriate after this caption. We are going to be shown things exactly as they occurred, aren't we? The screen fades to white and the non-diegetic music continues quietly. A bird flutters around as if behind gauze, and production company credits appear. A second instrument joins in with the solemn tune and a little gentle, bell-like percussion is added. Two points of light appear, resolving themselves into car headlights as if in mist or fine snow. The stars' names appear and fade. The car becomes clearer and drives towards the camera along a long, straight but undulating road. As it dips down, it disappears to reappear on the next rise, as an ominous drum beats and the full orchestra joins in with the dirge-like theme. The

Jerry meets the kidnappers
in a bar in Fargo: an anxious,
middle-aged man

car comes nearer to and past the camera and we see that it is pulling a trailer. The screen is filled with snow. The film's title *Fargo* fades up, white on nearly white. We see the car from the side, then from the rear as it drives away down the snowy road. It is towing another car through the bleak and bleary air and the picture fades. A caption announces 'Fargo, North Dakota'. The first action scene locates us outside a diner at night, and the car towing the second car which we have just seen is arriving. Diegetic country music plays on a jukebox and as we cut to the interior of the diner, an anxious, middle-aged man in hat and bulky anorak enters. It is Jerry.

```
The bar is downscale even for this town. Country
music plays on the jukebox.

Two men are seated in a booth at the back. One is
short, slight, youngish. The other man is somewhat
older, and dour. The table in front of them is
littered with empty long-neck beer bottles. The
ashtray is full.

Anderson approaches.

Anderson

      I'm, uh, Jerry Lundegaard -

Younger man

      You're Jerry Lundegaard?

Jerry

      Yah, Shep Proudfoot said -

Younger man

      Shep said you'd be here at 7.30. What
      gives, man?

Jerry

      Shep said 8.30.
```

Younger man

> We been sitting here an hour. I've peed three times already.

Jerry

> I'm sure sorry. I - Shep told me 8.30. It was a mix-up, I guess.

Younger man

> Ya got the car?

Jerry

> Yah, you bet. It's in the lot there. Brand-new burnt umber Ciera.

Younger man

> Yeah, okay. Well, siddown, then. I'm Carl Showalter and this is my associate Gaear Grimsrud.

Jerry

> Yah, how ya doin'. So, uh, we all set on this thing, then?

Carl

> Sure, Jerry, we're all set. Why wouldn't we be?

Jerry

> Yah, no, I'm sure you are. Shep vouched for you and all. I got every confidence here in you fellas.

They stare at him. An awkward beat.

> ... So I guess that's it, then. Here's the keys -

Carl

> No, that's not it, Jerry.

Jerry

    ... Huh?

Carl

    The new vehicle, plus forty thousand dollars.

Jerry

    Yah, but the deal was, the car first, see,
    then the forty thousand, like as if it was the
    ransom. I thought Shep told you -

Carl

    Shep didn't tell us much, Jerry.

Jerry

    Well, okay, it's -

Carl

    Except that you were gonna be here at 7.30.

Jerry

    Yah, well, that was a mix-up, then.

Carl

    Yeah, you already said that.

Jerry

    Yah. But it's not a whole pay-in-advance deal.
    I give you a brand-new vehicle in advance and -

Carl

    I'm not gonna debate you Jerry.

Jerry

    Okay.

Carl

    I'm not gonna sit here and debate. I will say
    this, though: what Shep told us didn't make a
    whole lot of sense.

in a bit of trouble ...

Jerry

    Oh, no, it's real sound. It's all worked out.

Carl

    You want your own wife kidnapped?

Jerry

    Yah.

Carl stares. Jerry looks blankly back.

Carl

    ... You — my point is, you pay the ransom —
    what, eighty thousand bucks? — I mean, you
    give us half the ransom, forty thousand, you
    keep half. It's like robbing Peter to pay
    Paul, it doesn't make any —

Jerry

    Okay, it's — see, it's not me payin' the
    ransom. The thing is, my wife, she's wealthy —
    her dad, he's real well off. Now, I'm in a bit
    of trouble —

Carl

    What kind of trouble are you in, Jerry?

Jerry

    Well, that's, that's, I'm not gonna go inta,
    inta — see, I just need money. Now, her dad's
    real wealthy —

Carl

    So why don't you just ask him for the money?

Grimsrud, the dour man who has not yet spoken, now
softly puts in with a Swedish-accented voice:

Grimsrud

    Or your fucking wife, you know.

Carl

> Or your fucking wife, Jerry.

Jerry

> Well, it's all just part of this — they don't
> know I need it, see. Okay, so there's that.
> And even if they did, I wouldn't get it. So
> there's that on top, then. See, these're
> personal matters.

Carl

> Personal matters.

Jerry

> Yah. Personal matters that needn't, uh —

Carl

> Okay, Jerry. You're asking us to perform this
> mission, but you, you won't — uh, you won't —
> aw, fuck it, let's take a look at that Ciera.

This scene opens as a reconstruction might, with a caption, and ends with a fade to black, as a reconstruction scene might. In between it is constructed quite classically, with establishing wide shots of the diner, moving into closer shots of Jerry, Carl and Gaear, then shot/reverse shot for the conversation.

An examination of the opening of the film, (i.e. the title sequence and the first action scene) reveals, in a variety of ways, the following narrative information:

■ There is snow. Visibility is poor. A car is driving to Fargo, towing a tan Ciera. It arrives at a diner at night. A man meets two other men. So much is revealed by the action and the caption announcing that we are in Fargo

■ The theme music in the film's titles dictates that the mood is solemn and foreboding. The images in the title sequence impart a feeling of chill, isolation and loneliness. These cue us to be worried that something is going to go wrong

the seeds of what is to come

■ The country music in the diner sounds cheerful, but the conversation is threatening. A crime is being planned and the man in charge is not really in charge. We can see this in his expression, his nervousness, and by the fact that he is already showing himself to be someone who apologises, makes excuses and stammers, another cue to worry

■ Carl shows signs of aggression and greed in his dialogue and body language. Gaear is virtually silent, but his one line is aggressive and challenging. The two of them contrast in size, sound and demeanour

■ Jerry wants to get it all over and done with, and to leave. His anxiety is clearly communicated

As well as giving out information, this beginning also raises questions:

Will Carl and Gaear do the job or cheat Jerry, aggravating his financial problems?

What is Gaear really like?

What could go wrong with this plan?

What will happen to poor, pathetic Jerry?

Why can't he just ask his rich wife for money?

What is she like?

What has Jerry done to get into debt, and who is pressing for payment?

The opening of the film contains the seeds of what is to come. We have been told, shown and cued in various ways to watch out for the growth and development of those seeds. The rest of the film is expected to reveal this development and ultimately to conclude it. The narrative organises where and when these developments and revelations take place.

space & time

Space information is organised by the mise-en-scène. Things we see and hear within a shot tell us where we are, which town, which building and room or which exterior location, and what happens there. Time is organised by editing.

another Coen joke

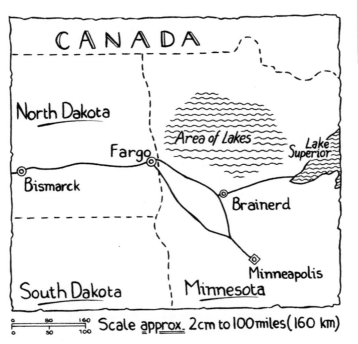

The spread out Fargo area

SPACE IN FARGO

Fargo is in North Dakota. A caption tells us so, in keeping with the film's pretensions to be a representation of what we have been told is a real-life story. No-one goes to Fargo again in the whole film, and no action other than the meeting of Jerry, Carl and Gaear takes place there. In fact, Fargo is hardly visited by the film and yet it is the title of the film, possibly another Coen joke (see Background: Director as Auteur and Context: Genre). It is, however, approximately a two hundred mile snowy drive from Minneapolis, which is in the neighbouring state of Minnesota. So when Jerry arrives home in time for supper and a caption tells us we are in Minneapolis in the second scene, we can be pretty sure that it is not still the same evening as that on which he met his two conspirators. We know it was already 8.30 when he met them and probably at night, since it was dark. From Minneapolis it is about a hundred miles to Brainerd, back towards Fargo and east a little.

Brainerd is signified by the grotesque papier-mâché figure of the legendary lumberjack, Paul Bunyan, and on an early visit there, the wording on the base of the figure, 'Welcome to Brainerd – home of Paul Bunyan' is lit up by headlights. The neon sign on the Blue Ox Motel which cashes in on the Bunyan legend, is also used to locate us in Marge Gunderson's territory, the Brainerd area. The first three murders take place in this area. Here too, the night before the kidnapping and first murders, Carl and Gaear, making a little detour en route from Fargo to Minneapolis, get laid by the two hookers at the Blue Ox Motel and their car with dealer plates is spotted. Also somewhere in the vicinity of Brainerd is the kidnappers' hide-out, though this is off the beaten track, since it is in the area searched by Marge near Moose Lake. Jean and Carl are killed here.

Minneapolis is the home of Jerry Lundegaard, therefore the place where the kidnapping takes place. When Carl and Gaear first arrive there, Carl points out some of its landmarks for Gaear and for us. Marge announces her intentions of going there to follow up the telephone call which leads to Shep's place, so when we later see her checking into a hotel, we know where we are. Wade and the car park attendant are killed in the Dayton-Radisson car park and Marge meets Mike Yanagita at the Radisson Hotel, in Minneapolis.

Bismarck is the place where Jerry is eventually captured, and is announced in a caption. This is about four hundred miles from Minneapolis, even beyond Fargo.

These places, then, are fairly spread out. In the snowy conditions it must have taken time to move between them. Knowing the distances helps the overall understanding of the slow, slippery slide into the mess and on towards the inevitable close of the story. It is not until we realise the distances between places involved in *Fargo* that the time scale can be appreciated. American audiences may know that Minneapolis is not just down the road from Fargo, but others may not. The timing of some of the events is caused by distance between places and probably by weather conditions, so that the story's events range over several days. Place is signalled in the dialogue, or in captions, or in the case of Brainerd by the figure of Paul Bunyan.

TIME IN FARGO

Time is organised by editing. The story of *Fargo* covers several days; the film takes less than two hours. It is quite clear that time has been compressed. What happens between shots is time. Where virtually no time elapses between shots, time is continuous. Where time does lapse there has been an ellipsis. In *Fargo*, ellipses are not always marked and have to be picked up from clues.

Time in which nothing has happened that the writer/director deems part of the action is left out. No-one wants to watch people sleep for eight hours! Such time is known as dead time. Sometimes a film makes it very clear that time has passed using perhaps a fade. But *Fargo* has few of these obvious indicators and may use the mise-en-scène to give information about time. There are time clues in television programmes: well-known daytime or evening shows are seen or heard in rooms in which action takes place e.g. the kidnapping of Jean, the murder of Carl. Day and night-time are also apparent when the sky can be seen. Almost at the end of the film, as Marge speaks to her colleague Lou on her radio, we learn that the kidnapping and the first murders took place 'last Wednesday'. Mr Mohra, (the man who gives information to another of Marge's colleagues, Gary, about a 'kinda funny-lookin" little guy who has been bragging about having killed someone and who claims to be staying up at the lake), says that he met this funny little guy 'last Tuesday'. We might assume that, if the kidnapping did not happen until Wednesday, Carl, Gaear and Jean had been holed up at Moose Lake for almost a week, time enough for the gregarious Carl, who likes female company, to be going a little stir-crazy. Add to such clues the understanding of distances between the locations, and you probably come up with a time scale like the one which follows (bearing in mind that events are in chronological order and there are no flashes back or forward and that we, the audience, see all relevant events):

Day 1 Jerry meets Carl and Gaear at 8.30 to set up the kidnapping

space & time

Day 2 Jerry arrives back home for supper with Jean, Wade and Scotty

Day 3 (An unspecified time after day two) Carl and Gaear set off for Minneapolis. Jerry sells the car to the couple who don't want TruCoat. Carl and Gaear get laid at the Blue Ox Motel

Day 4 Jean reprimands Scotty for getting weak grades and Wade phones to say he likes Jerry's parking lot idea. Jerry visits Shep Proudfoot to try to get a phone number so he can forestall the kidnapping. Carl and Gaear, arguing about lack of conversation, arrive in Minneapolis. At work Jerry talks nervously to his loan company on the phone. The kidnapping takes place. Jerry, Wade and Stan Grossman the accountant discuss the parking lot deal and Jerry is bitterly disappointed by what is to be his share. He arrives home with the 'growsheries' in a bag for Jean, discovers the kidnapping and phones Wade. At this point it is still light, but later, in darkness, we see the first three murders take place on a straight, deserted road. This then, has been Wednesday

Day 5 Chief Marge Gunderson is called out of her bed to the murder investigation. Jerry, Wade and Stan discuss what to do about the kidnapping in a cafe. Jerry goes home to talk to his son. Carl and Gaear arrive at the cabin by the lake, with the hooded Jean, who runs around like a headless chicken. Norm brings Marge burgers for lunch at the police station. She gives him his night-crawlers. Lou comes in with the lead on the tan Ciera at the Blue Ox. Marge interviews the two hookers who say that Carl and Gaear had been heading for Minneapolis. Later, as the two murderers try to make the television set work in the cold cabin, the camera zooms in on the malfunctioning screen, and out again on the Gunderson's television screen. Marge and Norm watch a nature programme from their beds, drowsily. We can see that the two events are concurrent. Mike Yanagita calls. It is 10.45

Day 6 Jerry is at work when Carl calls to say that the price of the job has gone up, because three people are dead. The loan company call to say they are about to start legal proceedings. Jerry flips a little. Marge and Norm eat a huge lunch. A colleague brings Marge information about phone calls made from the Blue Ox to Minneapolis the night that the murderers stayed there, one being to Shep Proudfoot. That night, Jerry, Wade and Stan eat at

FARGO

Jerry's home. Wade insists on being the one to take the ransom money to the kidnappers

Day 7 Marge is in Minneapolis following the Shep Proudfoot lead. She is staying in the Radisson Hotel. Carl drives onto a near empty, snowy rooftop parking lot and swaps plates on the Ciera for someone else's. On leaving, he argues with the car park attendant over four dollars. Marge visits Shep at work; he says almost nothing. Jerry is visiting Shep too, but is scared off when he sees Marge. Later Marge visits Jerry as the representative of a company employing Shep, which might possibly own the tan Ciera with dealer plates. He says no cars are missing. Later Marge has a drink with Mike Yanagita. Carl takes a hostess/hooker to see Jose Feliciano, then back to Shep's home. Shep bursts in on them. Carl threatens Jerry by phone and Wade leaves immediately with the ransom money. Jerry follows. Wade is shot dead by Carl who is wounded in the jaw by Wade, but makes off with the money. Jerry hides Wade's body in the boot of Wade's own car and Carl shoots the car park attendant. Jerry goes to bed

Day 8 Gary sees the informant Mr Mohra, who puts him onto the lake hide-out. Carl hides most of the money. Marge discovers by phone that Mike Yanagita is weird. Marge interviews Jerry again, he panics and flees. Carl arrives back at the cabin. He and Gaear fall out over who gets the car. Gaear has shot Jean off screen. He kills Carl with an axe. Marge, driving round Moose Lake and talking on the radio with Lou, sees the Ciera, captures Gaear and takes him in

Sometime later, maybe on another day, maybe not, Jerry is caught in Bismarck, four hundred miles away. Norm's painting has won the honour of being on the three cent stamp and Marge and Norm settle down for the night, looking forward to the birth of their baby

The compression of time is all done by omitting the unimportant. By and large there is a strong causal link between any scene and earlier and later scenes. And it is the characters and their motivation which are the causes. Some scenes which are not directly relevant to the crime story are, however, included, probably because they give character information.

Marge's drink with Mike Yanagita has nothing to do with the story, nor has Jerry's attempt to sell TruCoat. It requires careful reading and analysis to follow in detail what is happening when, but the chronological organisation of events ensures that we can follow the story for pleasure well enough without needing to know exactly how time is passing. A classical narrative would have indicated all lapses of time and orientated viewers as to time and place at the start of each scene. Today's sophisticated viewers are expected to pick up information at a glance, without even being aware that they are doing so.

The mise-en-scène and editing organise and reveal the where and the when of events. The why can be found in examining characters and their motivation.

character

It is often a film's hero whose motives drive the film along. It is also quite common for the motives of forces opposing the hero to cause events to happen. The motives of the two opposing forces of good and evil are extremely common causal agents. But Marge does not cause much herself, until the very end, when her detective work causes Jerry to flee, and until she captures Gaear. Events in *Fargo* are caused by several people, but not the heroine, until almost the end of the film. Marge follows. Her motives are professional, not personal. The following people, however, do cause events:

■ Jerry initiates the events by setting up the kidnapping of Jean

■ Carl and Gaear cause many of the film's events by carrying out that task. They then have motives of their own which are causal as they try to avoid being caught for having done the deed. Their incompatibility is signalled early as they have problems conversing and this cues us to expect problems with this partnership

```
CAR
Carl is driving. Grimsrud stares out the front.
After a beat:
```

Margo takes aim:
the end of the road
for Gaear

Carl, the kinda funny looking
guy, turns nasty with a gun

Carl

    ... Look at that. Twin Cities. IDS Building, the big glass one. Tallest skyscraper in the Midwest. After the Sears, uh, Chicago ... You never been to Minneapolis?

Grimsrud

    No.

Carl

    ... Would it kill you to say something?

Grimsrud

    I did.

Carl

    'No.' First thing you've said in the last four hours. That's a, that's a fountain of conversation, man. That's a geyser. I mean, whoa, daddy, stand back, man. Shit, I'm sittin' here driving, man, doin' all the driving, whole fucking way from Brainerd, drivin', tryin' to, you know, tryin' to chat, keep our spirits up, fight the boredom of the road, and you can't say one fucking thing just in the way of conversation.

Grimsrud smokes, gazing out the window.

    ... Well, fuck it, I don't have to talk either, man. See how *you* like it.

Carl looks at Grimsrud for a reaction.

    ... Just total fuckin' silence. Two can play at *that* game, smart guy. We'll just see how *you* like it ...

He drives
... Total silence ...

■ Wade causes events by opposing Jerry's wishes

■ Even Mike Yanagita causes an event: a whole scene (his own reunion with Marge), but it has no causal link in the chain which links other events

■ Marge follows in the wake of the others. She is emotionally uninvolved. Everything is done as part of a day's work. She can almost be seen as an effect rather than a cause

The detective in a crime story often starts out just doing the job, but it is very common for the detective to become involved, possibly emotionally, with another character and almost certainly in the web of deceit and in the violence. Not Marge Gunderson. Her emotional life is at home. Marge is the eye of the storm, the still centre around which everything spins whilst she remains firmly anchored. In keeping with the film's claim to be a true story, this detective just detects and then only when at work. In fact all police work is seen as routine, not as action-packed heroism.

If characters and their motivation provide a drive through the story, themes i.e. underlying ideas which the story seems to be exploring, can also act as a narrative drive.

theme as structural device

It is common for a murder story to withhold a piece of vital evidence – an important causal link – from the viewers until the end of the film, in order to create mystery and/or suspense. But *Fargo* shows us everything. There is no mystery. The thrilling (or chilling) moments of the film are when the state trooper stops the tan Ciera and asks Carl for his tags; the scene on the rooftop car park when Wade takes on Carl as the bungling Jerry approaches; and when Marge, pregnant and vulnerable, confronts the dreadful Gaear by the wood chipper in the snow, then copes perfectly. This is an anticlimax quite daring for an American popular film. Only some aspects of the film's style (see Style) stand between it and the reconstruction of a true story which its form and narrative structures certainly resemble. The theme of good against evil provides a narrative drive because we have certain expectations, based on a frequent acquaintance with good-bad battles. We expect them to be resolved and the probability is that good will prevail, not necessarily because it does in life, but because it does in stories.

THE PRESSURE TO SUCCEED

This is a theme which runs through several, if not all Coen movies. The drive for the perfect life can be a negative drive, that is into crime. As in many gangster and crime films, the will to succeed can translate into some kind of perversion of the American Dream. For Jerry, who discovers that hard work and being married to the boss's daughter still do not gain him the status he craves, crime becomes the only answer. Marge and Norm are content with modest successes. They will never be criminals. We watch to discover who will win.

FAILURE TO CONSIDER OTHERS

Jerry, Carl and Gaear all make plans which involve other people, but which are intended primarily to benefit themselves. They do not consider that others are doing the same thing. There are seen to be problems stemming from the use of other people without the consideration of them as people with their own goals. Marge and Norm, however, do not exploit anyone and are mutually considerate and supportive of each other. Our desire to see them all get what they deserve keeps us engaged with the narrative.

The fact that an audience is engaged with the actions and motives of characters and the exploration of themes suggests that some kind of resolution is expected as a conclusion to what the film is all about.

THE CLOSE

By the time the film ends, all the questions posed by the film's opening (and a few raised along the way) are answered. We have complete closure. Everything which was disrupted has reached a new equilibrium. Some disrupted lives have ended in death. Jerry and Gaear have been brought to book and Marge is back at home in bed with Norm, talking about stamps and babies. It has been, as Marge would say, 'a real shame', though surely not quite a tragedy. Yet if we extend our consideration of the film to include the very end of the final credits, and notice there the previously mentioned declaration that the characters and events in the film are entirely fictitious, we may still wonder to whom this 'true' story of 'fictional' events happened! Could it be a tongue in cheek, semi-documentary style representation of something as true as one of those urban myths we hear about? Perhaps that is one question left unresolved.

style

signifiers of the real *p42*   **realism** *p43*   **signifiers of comedy** *p43*
film blanc? *p49*

The most important aspect of *Fargo*'s style is the fact that, in some respects, it mimics some documentary reconstruction forms which aim to tell a story from real life in an apparently straightforward, objective way. It is this mix of the objective style we have come to associate with reconstruction, with the far from objective humorous take on stories we have come to associate with the Coen Brothers, which is at the root of this film's style.

In order to appreciate the relative detachment of *Fargo*'s style, it may be helpful to know a few things about other Coen brothers' movies which have a less detached style. Possibly the most obvious (one might say flamboyant) examples of Coen style are in *Raising Arizona, The Hudsucker Proxy* and *The Big Lebowski*. There is something of the slapstick in these films, something about some people, some shots or scenes, some lines of wisecracking dialogue, which slaps you on the back and says, 'Only joking!' It may have something to do with the pace at which outrageous events occur, or that a camera angle is odd, off-balance, eccentric or self aware. It may be that there is something about a shot which recalls comic-book pictures, like the fall from the skyscraper building in *The Hudsucker Proxy*, or which harks back to famous comedians of the past such as Harold Lloyd, balancing precariously on a flagpole high above the street. It may be that there is something surreal going on, e.g. the lone, avenging biker who pursues the baby kidnappers on his Harley, with a pair of baby shoes dangling from his belt in *Raising Arizona*. It may be that a character is so stereotypical, that we know she or he is a parody, like the arrogant Latino bowling opponent of The Dude who struts and preens like the archetypal Spanish flamenco dancer in *The Big Lebowski*, so that we know not to take him seriously. Dream sequences feature amusingly in many Coen movies. There are many elements which signify a remove from the real.

Fargo, on the other hand, goes out of its way to assure us that it represents the real. Yet still it is funny. This is a story of violence and greed where only the good can resolve the situation by combating the evil. And it claims to be true. How can this be funny? Critics of Coen movies often damn them as cold, cynical and heartless, though most find *Fargo* more humane than earlier examples.

It is necessary to try to identify what the elements are which signify the real, and what elements there are which signify that it is all right to laugh. What is there which still creates that remove from real life and says: 'It's a film. It's for fun'?

signifiers of the real

Firstly, we have a declaration which holds that the events in the film happened in real life. Secondly we have elements of style which could bear that out:

■ The film takes place in real towns, on location. Scenes take place in real diners and real hotels. Minnesotans might recognise these

■ The camera style is less obtrusive than in other Coen films, quieter, if camera work can be quiet. It is more classical, draws less attention to itself and appears to be there only to expose the facts, the story. Shots are usually long shots, showing characters in their surroundings, with close ups used to emphasise the importance of the way a character is thinking or feeling at that moment. The camera is usually still

■ Dialogue is much slower than in previous Coen films where it flashes with wit and cleverness as it zips along. In *Fargo* it is less artificial and moves like the folks in the snow, slowly and carefully. Of course, it uses the local dialect and this has a dual function; it fits in with the realism and it signifies certain character attributes such as homeliness, lack of guile, lack of quick-wittedness and a certain dullness. It is a country accent as opposed to a city-slicker's accent with all the connotations that go along with 'country'

■ The film's heroine, Marge, is a genuinely good, average person. Most Coen heroes and heroines are engaged in dodgy dealings, one way or another, and we are attracted to them despite ourselves. Marge is just a nice, hard-working, honest everywoman, maybe even a bore, but she wins, and she and her home life get the last scene and the last word

■ Marge's attitude, that crime is a real shame, is actually the bottom line of the film's attitude to the crimes and the violence. It is a shame, but in the end, most of us go home like Marge, to bed, untouched by it and more interested in the lives of ourselves and our families. That is the only way that most of us can cope with ideas of terrible violence

realism

Realism is a complex subject, around which there are many debates. There are some who feel that it is morally wrong to lead audiences to believe that a story might be true, or that a text is revealing things exactly as they happened, if there is any room for doubt at all. Some films take a historical story as a basis and manipulate the feelings of the audience to respond in a given way to that story. Even having a popular star to play the role of a real person manipulates how audiences feel about the role, therefore about the person. Many dislike any truth-fact-fiction confusion (witness the controversy generated by *The Blair Witch Project*, Myrick and Sanchez, 1998). On the other hand, some feel that film makers should say anything they want in any style and that audiences should read film intelligently and make up their own minds. The Coens are well aware of these debates, as most modern film makers are, and they appear to be deliberately courting controversy, albeit of a light-hearted nature. It must be stressed that realism is not an absence of style. It is as deliberately adopted as any other style for the meaning it conveys. It is nonetheless a concept, a representation of the real by the reel.

signifiers of comedy

This is a much more difficult set of signifiers to identify, because humour itself is such a shifting, elusive thing, and there is nothing so unfunny as the explained joke. There are people who find nothing to laugh at whatsoever in *Fargo* or who feel that the Coens are laughing in a very unpleasant manner at people like Marge and Norm. Some disagree and feel that to laugh at this couple means that we are laughing at ourselves, or at the Coens' ability to show us how funny normal life can be. But it is possible to identify what may be the source of some of the humour, and some will agree that it makes for comedy. The comedy here, though, is not slapstick. It is far more subtle and is very black:

■ The juxtaposition of dreadful violence with Marge's unshakeable normality can be funny. When she sees the very first murder victims and throws up right afterwards, it is because she has morning sickness and not because of the blood. Conversation with Lou immediately turns to breakfast, eggs and Norm. She is vulnerable, yet placid and confident. It is both realistic and incongruous

■ Marge's capacity for food runs through the whole film. Her next meal is far more important than her next clue. She is eating for two without a doubt. This is a big leap from the detective we are used to in crime drama, who never eats, possibly is only ever seen to consume hard liquor, or who is so bound up with the pursuit that food is not important. In the police department's time, and between meal breaks, without a single miscalculation, Marge finds the criminals and captures them. She, being so unstereotypical, raises our awareness of what was stereotypical. She is a deconstruction of the detective in crime fiction film

■ Jerry is also a realistic character, but he does something way beyond the scope of most of us. Again we have the juxtaposition of the realistic with the gross and the melodramatic. We must all know people like Jerry who long to be successful but have neither the talent nor the luck for it. He is like many people, but Jerry takes a huge step into another world and is pathetically unable to cope. What is funny is that the audience can see everything coming. Jerry cannot. We groan as we laugh

■ The stereotypical psychopathic murderers, Carl and Gaear on the other hand, cannot be said to be like people we meet every day. They work the other way round. They are characters from murder and crime stories who, when thrust into the downbeat, sad little realistic world of the pathetic Jerry, behave in a grossly over-the-top way suitable only for the horror genre or a Coen brothers' movie

■ The contrasting physical appearance of the murderers to one another, and the fact that the little dark one talks continuously whilst the big blond says next to nothing, gives them something of the air of the double act: the straight man and the stooge, Laurel and Hardy, the dumb-blond-with-

FARGO

Domestic bliss: Margo and Norm
with burgers and night-crawlers

a-difference and the little mad macho guy. It is superficial contrast. Inside they are both psychopaths. If such people do exist in real life they would not be funny. Carl and Gaear are

■ Costume is used for humour. The best example of this is the scene in which Mr Mohra gives information about the lakeside hideout to Gary, the cop. Both wear hooded parkas. It is funny because this informant/ bartender is so unlike those we have met before in crime film. Marge wearing her cardigan in bed is also amusing because, when heroines are seen in bed with a partner, sex rather than comfort is usually being signalled. Not for Marge and Norm. Marge's big woolly mittens worn along with her gun have the same comic effect

■ Minnesota as a setting is exploited for humour, too. Certainly if the town of Brainerd were truly the setting for these horrific murders, then it is a happy comic coincidence, brain + nerd. Minnesota's snow slows things down, throws people off balance, makes them dress stupidly. It makes a terrified, hooded kidnap victim's dash for freedom look ridiculous, the dash of the headless chicken! It exposes the stupidity of the cunning and avaricious Carl, as he buries the ransom money in snow, looks round (after the event) to see if anyone has seen him, then realises there are miles of identical fence posts in the snow, and sticks a little, probably ineffectual marker next to his stash. The snow, like everything else in his life, is there to make Jerry Lundegaard's life harder, too. He has to drive through it pulling a trailer. He has to get the groceries in whilst his wife, Jean, probably habitually stays home. It messes up his car windscreen just when he can least handle yet another complication

■ Minnesota's locals with surnames of Scandinavian origin are exploited for humour, evoking memories of cartoon characters like Bullwinkle the Moose, Elmer Fudd and the hurdy-gurdy chef in *The Muppet Show*

■ Anticlimax, or bathos is used to great effect. Examples are usually connected with dialogue. When Marge examines the murdered state trooper, the first victim – whose frozen, dead face we have seen in close up in the foreground of a shot so that we cannot escape it – she stands, claps the snow from her woolly-mittened hands and remarks that 'It's a real shame.' Jerry says, 'Oh, geez!' or 'Heck!' in response to any bad news, no matter how nasty. But the best example of anticlimax of all is not in the dialogue. It is in the action. We watch, fearful for the pregnant Marge's safety, as she calls out to Gaear, stuffing his partner into the wood chipper. He throws a log at her and runs. Perhaps he does not have his axe or a gun with him, because Marge simply has to fire to wound him and he is brought down, helpless. In the back of her car and handcuffed securely, Gaear is ticked off by Marge about the consequences of greed

■ There are two characters in the film who say almost nothing, Gaear and Shep. Shep is supposed to have recommended Gaear to Jerry for the kidnapping of Jean. One is left wondering how these two grunters ever fell into conversation in the first place, this dumb blond and the Indian who will barely speak to Marge

```
INSIDE THE CUBICLE
Marge
        - Wednesday night?
Shep is shaking his head.
Shep
        Nope.
Marge
        Well, you do reside there at 1425
        Fremont Terrace?
Shep
        Yep.
Marge
        Anyone else residing there?
Shep
        Nope.
Marge
        Well, Mr Proudfoot, this call came in past
        three in the morning. It's just hard for
```

```
        me to believe you can't remember anyone
        calling.
Shep says nothing.
        ... Now, I know you've had some problems,
        struggling with the narcotics, some other
        entanglements, currently on parole -
Shep
        So?
Marge
        Well, associating with criminals, if you're
        the one they talked to, that right there would
        be a violation of your parole and would end
        you up back in Stillwater.
Shep
        Uh-huh.
Marge
        Now, I saw some rough stuff on your priors,
        but nothing in the nature of a homicide ...
Shep stares at her.
        ... I know you don't want to be an accessory
        to something like that.
Shep
        Nope.
Marge
        So you think you might remember who those
        folks were who called ya?
```

Apart from the humour derived largely from the interaction of elements which signify everyday humdrum realism and those which signify exceptional horror and violent genres, there are other aspects of style worth noting.

film blanc?

Most people who have an interest in film will have come across the term film noir. Some refer to the film noir genre, others see it as a style adopted in the making of detective and gangster film, rather than as a genre in itself. *Fargo* is a crime story of murder and deceit. After that has been said, there is nothing more of the noir about it. Indeed, it is almost as if the Coens had looked at a list of film noir characteristics and gone for the direct opposite in every case. It is like a film noir negative!

FILM NOIR STEREOTYPES

■ Mysterious, beautiful women whose motives are not made clear until the end of the film, often referred to as a *femme fatale*

■ Hard-bitten, streetwise, often witty male detectives with a cynical edge, no family and no ties

■ Neat, sweet wives or mother figures in secondary roles

■ Smooth criminals or psychologically disturbed killers

■ The appearance of bartenders, journalists and informers

STEREOTYPES IN FARGO

■ There is no woman in *Fargo* who comes anywhere near the stereotypical *femme fatale*. Jean Lundegaard is never seen outside a domestic situation, until after her kidnap, then she has a bag on her head. She is seen cooking, dealing with her· son and knitting. She wears jogging bottoms and cardigans. Marge favours cardigans, too, and woolly hats and mittens. She is seen in domestic settings, at work and out in the bright snow. She is pregnant and she is plain. She has no mystery. The nearest she comes to a *femme fatale* scene is her drink with Mike Yanagita where she is patently embarrassed by the interest he claims to have in her, and retreats behind her diet coke with a straw. Even the two bouncy, pleasant, rather innocent hookers at the Blue Ox are wholesome local girls, one of whom went to college and supports the local team. 'Go, Bears!' she says in the film (though not in the screenplay). Carl's hostess date at the Jose Feliciano concert may try to look a little *fatale*, but ends up stark naked running from a furious Shep

■ *Fargo* has no streetwise, hard-bitten male detective. It has a uniformed, pregnant female cop on a rare murder case. Marge cannot pull her hat down over her eyes. She could pull the flaps down over her ears but the effect would be different. Although she is shrewd and alert, Marge is not cynical or witty; her conversation is centred around food and Norm. Marge has no reason to want to fool anyone, or appear other than she is, or to say anything other than directly. She has no hidden motives

■ The two wives who appear in the film are Jean, who is also a mother and Marge who is about to be. Both roles are crucial. Jean is frumpy, shrill and also a murder victim. She is seen exclusively in the home until kidnapped. Marge is not a secondary character, but is Chief Gunderson, seen both at home and at work, at the very heart of the film

■ The criminals in *Fargo* are about as far from smooth as is possible. They are disorganised, wild and amoral. They quite probably are psychopathic, but we are never treated to a look into their psyche. Whatever is behind their actions is not dealt with in the film. Psychoanalysis is not built in

■ Bartenders feature only minimally as characters in *Fargo*, since there are so few bar or nightclub scenes. Mr Mohra tends a bar, as he tells Gary, the cop, when reporting his suspicions about the lakeside hideaway. That is why he has conversed with Carl. But we do not see him *in situ*. We see him sweeping up the snow on his drive, in his hooded parka. He is spoken to politely and addressed as 'Mr Mohra'. There are no creepy little informers, and no journalists

Amongst the characters then, there is a detective, there are criminals, there are women and there are peripheral roles like hookers and a bartender, but each of these is so unlike those in the noir style thriller, that it could be said that either this is really a true story – hence the accidental absence of stereotypes – or the Coens are being deliberately as un-noir about the style of this thriller as they can.

A similar conclusion might be reached about the visual style of *Fargo*.

THE VISUAL STYLE OF FILM NOIR

■ A large proportion of night-time scenes

■ Dark, claustrophobic, urban settings

■ Few scenes in natural settings and natural light, or of domesticity

■ An emphasis on scenes set in bars, nightclubs and hotel rooms, each artificially lit

■ Unbalanced framing of shots used to disorientate the viewer and to convey insecurity

■ A lighting style of high contrast, using areas of light and dark very effectively

■ The voyeuristic camera, watching the *femme fatale*'s every move, whenever she is present

■ An overall expressionism pervading the visual style to communicate emotions like fear and suspicion and a sense of mystery

THE VISUAL STYLE OF FARGO

■ Much of the action of the film takes place in the daytime, when Jerry is at work, or in a brightly lit kitchen, police station, hotel lobby or cafeteria with no dark corners. *Fargo*'s characters are not creatures who lurk in the shadows and only come out at night. The working day seems to be the time at which the majority of events take place. There are nine really bright, white daytime scenes in the snow:

1 Jerry in the parking lot

2 Marge investigating the first murders

3 Jean's headless chicken dash at the cabin

4 Jerry selling a car at work

5 Carl in a parking lot, swapping car number plates

6 Mr Mohra's information to Gary

7 Carl burying the money by the fence in the snow

8 Marge driving round the lake and capturing Gaear

9 Gaear's attack on Carl

The film's title sequence is also bright and snowy, but also rather misty.

film blanc?

■ There is a wide-open, rural feel to *Fargo*, rather than a claustrophobic urban feel. The sense of light and space more closely resembles that in a Western than that in a noir thriller. Although towns are settings for events, they do not press down on the characters, do not threaten them by holding hidden horrors in their dark corners. We see them in broad daylight

■ A quick tally reveals that there are only about seven night scenes, which actually look dark:

1 The arrival of Jerry towing the Ciera in Fargo at the diner

2 Carl and Gaear with the two hookers at the Blue Ox

3 The first three murders all in one sequence

4 Marge's first scene

5 Carl's night out to see Jose Feliciano

6 Carl with the hooker at Shep's flat

7 The murder of Wade and wounding of Carl

■ There are many domestic and natural settings for the action in *Fargo* as well as the urban settings. Jerry's home is shown several times as is that of Marge and Norm's. Even when Carl and Gaear need a hide-out for their kidnap victim, they select one in a natural, rural setting by a lake, rather than a one lost in a maze of city streets. Natural daylight is the most usual source of light in *Fargo*

■ There is no emphasis on artificially lit bars, hotels and nightclubs. Indeed the opposite can be said. There is an emphasis on naturally lit homes and places of legitimate work. The characters are largely stable with a fixed abode, so they do not inhabit hotels, motels or temporary accommodation. Only Marge stays at a hotel, and we know that this is unusual for her because she is worried where her meals will come from. When she visits a bar, it is not to peer with veiled eyes through her cigarette smoke, but to sip a diet coke with an old school friend

■ The framing of shots are never skewed for effect. Composition is balanced so that it appears to be nothing out of the ordinary. No attention is drawn to it and the viewer's positioning as unseen witness to events is objective, the evidence never being emotionally loaded by off-centre framing. If we take a scene in which it is obvious that Jerry is scared, panicking and feeling threatened, and examine how that scene is shot, it will become apparent just how objective the style is, how little the emotions are led by the nature of the shots

```
Marge sticks her head in the door.

Marge
        Mr Lundegaard? Sorry to bother you again. Can
        I come in?

She starts to enter.

Jerry
        Yah, no, I'm kinda - I'm kinda busy -

Marge
        I unnerstand. I'll keep it real short, then.
        I'm on my way out of town, but I was just - Do
        you mind if I sit down? I'm carrying a bit of
        a load here.

Jerry
        No, I -

But she is already sitting into the chair opposite
with a sigh of relieved weight.

Marge
        Yah, it's this vehicle I asked you about
        yesterday. I was just wondering -

Jerry
        Yah, like I told ya, we haven't had any
        vehicles go missing.

Marge
Okay, are you sure, 'cause, I mean, how do you
know? Because, see, the crime I'm investigating,
the perpetrators were driving a car with dealer
plates. And they called someone who works here, so
it'd be quite a coincidence if they weren't, ya
know, connected.
```

I answered your question

Jerry

Yah, I see.

Marge

So how do you — have you done any kinda
inventory recently?

Jerry

The car's not from our lot, ma'am.

Marge

But do you know that for sure without —

Jerry

Well, I would know. I'm the Executive Sales
Manager.

Marge

Yah, but —

Jerry

We run a pretty tight ship here.

Marge

I know, but — well, how do you establish that,
sir? Are the cars, uh, counted daily, or what
kind of —

Jerry

Ma'am, I answered your question.

There is a silent beat.

Marge

... I'm sorry, sir?

Jerry

Ma'am, I answered your question. I answered
the darn — I'm cooperating here, and I ...

Marge

Sir, you have no call to get snippy with me.
I'm just doin' my job here.

Jerry

    I'm not, uh, I'm not arguin' here. I'm
    cooperating ... There's no, uh — we're doin'
    all we can ...

He trails off into silence.

Marge

    Sir, could I talk to Mr Gustafson?

Jerry stares at her.

    ... Mr Lundegaard?

Jerry explodes:

Jerry

    Well, heck, if you wanna, if you wanna play
    games here! I'm workin' with ya on this thing,
    but I ...

He is getting angrily to his feet.

    ... Okay, I'll do a damned lot count!

Marge

    Sir? Right now?

Jerry

    Sure right now! You're darned tootin'!

He is yanking his parka from a hook behind the
opened door and grabbing a pair of galoshes.

    ... If it's so damned important to ya!

Marge

    I'm sorry, sir, I —

Jerry has the parka slung over one arm and the
galoshes pinched in his hand.

Jerry

    Aw, what the Christ!

He stamps out the door. Marge stares. After a long
moment her stare breaks. She glances idly around the
office.

There is a framed picture facing away from her on
the desktop. She turns it to face her. It is
Scotty, holding an accordion. There is another
picture of Jean.

Marge looks at it, looks around, looks, for some
reason, at the ceiling.

She looks at a trophy shelf on the wall behind her.

She fiddles idly with a pencil. She pulls a
clipboard toward her. It holds a form from the
General Motors Finance Corporation.

She looks idly around. Her look abruptly locks.

Marge

     ... Oh, for Pete's sake.

Jerry is easing his car around the near corner of
the building.

Marge's voice is flat with dismay:

     ... Oh, for Pete's sake ...

She grabs the phone and punches in a number.

     ... For Pete's s — he's fleein' the interview.
     He's fleein' the interview ...

Jerry makes a left turn into traffic.

     ... Detective Sibert, please ...

This is the second time Marge interviews Jerry in his office about the tan
Ciera and Marge is sure that there is a connection between the murderers,
Shep and this car salesroom. She has no suspicions, however, about Jerry
personally and only suspects that the car has been stolen from there. It is
a puzzle to her why Jerry is so unco-operative about going and checking
to see if anything is missing. Jerry, on the other hand, is guilty and
therefore afraid that Marge has worked out more than she has. He is
frightened enough to lose his composure and flee.

In a noir thriller, his fast beating heart and his spinning, frightened head would be revealed to us by style; music, lighting, composition and camera angle or movement would tell us. Marge's power over Jerry might be conveyed by off-centre framing and a camera angle exaggerating her height in relation to his as she stands over him. But in *Fargo* it is not so. When Jerry is first seen in this sequence, he is doodling with the figures of car serial numbers, trying to fudge them again. We see first his hands, then him in close up. We cut as Marge in long shot enters the office and walks towards him. Jerry in close up looks up as she speaks to him. As they converse, a classic shot/reverse shot edit is used to alternate looking over Jerry's shoulder as Marge speaks, and vice versa. Framing is consistent with the straightforward classic framing of such shots: Marge is slightly to the right of the frame in her shots, Jerry equally to the left in his. Marge is polite, pleasant, direct. Jerry is a little flustered. There is a pause and a subtle change as Marge stands and points out that she is only doing her job, that Jerry has no call to be 'snippy' with her. The pause and her rise to her feet are enough to convince the guilt-ridden Jerry that she is onto him. He looks up at her standing there, but there is no exaggeration of their relative height or power, no looming, no fish-eye lenses to distort reality, just a simple medium two shot. Then he jams on his hat and leaves, ostensibly to do a lot count, but really to flee.

Marge, left alone in his office, looks about her and, glancing slightly over her shoulder in case anyone is looking, she takes a glimpse at the papers on his desk. On realising that Jerry has fled, she calls her colleagues for help. Her activity after Jerry leaves the office is filmed with a static camera and she is in medium shot, producing an effect which resembles fly on the wall documentary, where the filmed person is unaware of the presence of a camera (here wasted on the respectful Marge)

■ The lighting in *Fargo* does not make use of the low-key lighting techniques so loved by makers of film noir. There is no use of high contrast with its very dark and very light areas. A shot is not dark for any meaning other than realism. A scene is only dark when it shows something happening at night, or in the case of Shep's garage, where little light gets in. Scenes are normally well lit in *Fargo*, even the corners. The example used above, of Marge interviewing Jerry, takes place before a large window in broad daylight. There is no attempt to make it look otherwise for reasons of atmosphere. It must be said though, that of the four murders which we see (three happen off camera), all take place at night, so there is still an association of dark and night and crime. Carl is killed in daylight. In *Fargo* there is no attempt to create a mystery. The function of the style of this film is to appear to be showing the facts as clearly and simply as possible. Even the shots from on high – e.g. of the almost empty car park into which Jerry walks to find his windscreen frozen – have a similar function, to establish where a scene is going to take place

■ Linked to other aspects of visual style is the fact that the camera does not follow around the heroine, Marge. She is not a mystery, so she can be allowed out of our sight. There is nothing voyeuristic about *Fargo*'s camera work, least of all around Marge. Marge is transparent, what you see is what you get. There is no need to keep your eyes on her

■ The absence of expressionism means that there is no obvious emotionalising of the story of *Fargo*. The polite distance of the nearly motionless camera watching objectively creates an illusion of lack of conscious style, a sense of just presenting the events. But realism is adopted just as consciously as expressionism. It is not unstylish. It is a deliberate style change for the Coens

FILM NOIR SOUND QUALITIES

■ Dialogue is slick, racy, urban slang

■ Characters deliver their lines guardedly, the women breathily with sidelong glances, the men cynically, concealing or seeming to conceal

■ Music is either very dramatic, pseudo-Wagnerian orchestral music, or nightclub jazzy

SOUND AND STYLE IN FARGO

■ One could hardly consider Jerry's mode of speech to be racy urban slang. It is slow and polite. Jean is shrill, but not racy and she and her husband are horrified to hear their son swear. When Jerry nervously flees from Marge, the most he can manage is an 'Aw, Heck!' Wade's style is a little more authoritative, but not racy and not slang. Marge and Norm have low voices and Marge says only what she means and only what she needs to

style

film blanc?

mad macho guy

just plain talking:
little mad macho guy

say, though having had to correct Lou's police work as he searches for a car registered DLR, she then jokes to cheer him up again. Lou is not witty, he is a little slow but plods reliably through police work to find some good leads. Indeed, the inhabitants of Minnesota, on the evidence of this film, are not slick, racy or witty in their speech. Their speech patterns belong perhaps to the Western genre, like the natural locations and the quality of light. The only fast talker is Carl, who is not from the area. His speech is wild and a little crazy, but his shot-up jaw joke, 'You should see the other guy!' is almost Philip Marlowe's standard

■ By and large the dialogue of *Fargo* is delivered directly, not murmured aside, or under the breath, nor huskily intimate. It is just plain talking. It seems to be a genuine if comical representation of the speech of this area, rather than the snappy dialogue usually associated with the Coens or the witticisms associated with some noir murder thrillers

■ There is no loud, dramatic, pseudo-Wagnerian orchestral music in *Fargo*. The most memorable music is the orchestral arrangement by regular Coen collaborator, Carter Burwell, of *The Lost Sheep*, an old Scandinavian folk tune and hymn. The simple tune is played at various times on different instruments for different effects. When played by the full orchestra, it swells into a wide, sweeping and stately tune, sometimes once again reminiscent of music one might find in a Western, and then again sometimes reminiscent of a slow, funereal march. Other music is diegetic, in keeping with the style of this film for realism, often as a sort of Muzak, so faint as to be utterly unobtrusive. Songs play on a jukebox. Jose Feliciano sings when Carl and the girl go to see a Feliciano performance

■ It could be said that sound effects also fall into the category of realism, that the squeaky scrunching of boots on snow is realistic, that the sound added to the fight scene between Shep and Carl is realistic. Certainly it is not unrealistic, not exaggerated, does nothing to draw attention to itself. But how many of us know what it sounds like to push a body through a wood chipper? That awful whining, moaning, mechanical noise sounds as though it might be realistic, but must come straight from the imagination of the sound effects department!

contexts

ideological *p61*   **cultural context** *p64*   **filmography** *p67*

genre *p70*   **production history** *p73*   **industrial context** *p76*

audience *p78*   **critical responses** *p82*

ideology

The Coen brothers began making feature films in the early Eighties, their first being released in 1984. This was a time of right wing, free market monetarism when the Republican Ronald Reagan was President of the USA. In 1987, Oliver Stone's *Wall Street* gave us the monstrous Gordon Gekko and his 'Greed is good!' credo, but Coen brothers' films never made heroes of wealthy or powerful people. *Fargo*, made right in the middle of the so-called 'nicer Nineties', continues the Coen tradition of favouring the less bullying, less manipulative and less avaricious members of society. In keeping with a change from the Eighties' dominant ideology of individual wealth-seeking, to the Nineties' more humane ideology under the presidency of the Democrat Bill Clinton, *Fargo* has more humanity and heart than the previous clever, witty but possibly colder Coen films.

STEREOTYPES AND VALUE JUDGEMENTS

A Coen brothers' hero or heroine is unlikely to be someone who yields great power. On the contrary, their protagonists are not rich and domineering but are often dominated by wealthy, successful, powerful men who are shown in an unsympathetic light. Each film has its bullying, scheming man who is more successful than the film's protagonists: Marty in *Blood Simple*; Nathan Arizona in *Raising Arizona* (whose motto is 'do it my way or watch your butt!'); Leo O'Bannion and Johnny Caspar, the rival mobsters in *Miller's Crossing*; Jack Lipnick the studio boss in *Barton Fink*; cigar smoking Sydney Mussburger in *The Hudsucker Proxy*; Jeff (not The Dude) Lebowski in *The Big Lebowski*; and of course Wade Gustafson in *Fargo*. Many of these characters come to very unpleasant ends.

By and large, in a Coen movie, the more relaxed and easy-going a character is, the more likely she or he is to survive. Marge in *Fargo* probably epitomises the type most likely to survive. For *Fargo* takes quite a risk in daring to make heroes of people so ordinary and unexceptional as to be boring! The qualities which are valued in this film are reliability, thoroughness in routine jobs, placidity, contentment, averageness and loyalty. People who have those qualities emerge as the winners. Marge gets the bad guys and is after all a police chief; Norm gets his painting on a stamp albeit one of small denomination; Lou finds lots of leads for Marge. Not one of them is ever under threat, even if for a moment or two we might think that Marge is.

On the other hand, the less laid back, the more avaricious and the more manic a character is, the more likely she or he might be to come to a dreadful end. Carl is archetypal, and think of the end that befalls him. He is greedy, stupid and violent, all qualities which are given negative value in the film. Steve Buscemi builds on previous roles such as Mr Pink in Tarantino's *Reservoir Dogs* for this stereotypical, amoral, macho murderer.

The qualities of ordinariness, then, are not equated with stupidity. It is the flashy, crazy or greedy stereotypes who behave stupidly. Carl buries the money where he would never find it again. Wade takes the ransom money and an inadequate gun to tackle the psychopathic Carl. Jerry makes mistake after mistake. Gaear and Shep are nearly speechless, probably mentally dull, and almost robotic. Gaear's image bears an increasing resemblance to the papier-mâché figure of Paul Bunyan as the film goes on. Marge, on the other hand – ordinary chief of ordinary police, the comfortable wife of comfortable Norm – is never stupid. She puts two and two together from the clues and the leads and gets exactly four. She draws her gun only once and when she has to fire it, hits her target right where she wants to, in the leg with the second shot. The only thing that Marge does not understand is that anyone should commit violent crime for financial gain. This lack of understanding is nothing to do with her intelligence. It is simply that Marge is a good, wholesome, incorruptible woman whose values have nothing whatever to do with being rich. Comfort is enough for Marge. She is paradoxical, slow of speech and movement but quick witted, a very ordinary woman but a very extraordinary heroine for American fiction.

In a similar way, Jerry is an unusual stereotype for masterminding a criminal plan. Here is another man in the street, neither sinister nor wild, nor threatening in any way. He is not clever, works in middle management, but is going nowhere and has no apparent talents. Yet Jerry is greedy and instigates the whole thing. He is last to be caught and that is significant, since conventionally it is the most terrible criminal who is last to be caught and who may need a positive hail of bullets to kill him. Jerry is dragged out of a motel room in his underpants, screaming. Mild-mannered, ordinary guys in American crime films are usually relegated to the role of witness or relative of a victim, and are not to be feared. Jerry manages to be both completely non-threatening and completely guilty. He is both criminal and victim, but not an innocent victim.

What the two folks-next-door, stereotypical Minnesotans Jerry and Marge do, is to make us smile at their unlikely situations and then, as we consider why they are so amusing, we are forced to contrast them with our expectations of cops and criminals. In noting that the last one to be caught is the least terrifying of the criminals, we are forced to realise that this is odd because it is not what we expect. Because they are both stereotypical Minnesotans in speech and manners, we also compare them with each other and realise that they could not be more different in character, despite superficial similarities.

FARGO, FAMILY AND SUBVERSIVE MEANING

It is not only the stereotypes of the thriller genre and the style and form of the thriller film which have been deconstructed by *Fargo*, but also the representation of the family. In this film, the patriarchal family unit in the capitalist world is seen as problematic. It actually causes the distress which causes the film. The patriarchal businessman, Wade, dominates his family whilst believing he is protecting them. He makes the weaker Jerry feel inadequate and because he is not only Jerry's employer, but also his father-in-law, Jerry feels inadequate both at work and at home. In fact he feels so bad that he is prepared to go to ridiculous lengths to gain some sort of respect. As a result, he loses everything and his family is destroyed. The family in which businessmen-fathers provide and rule is being subverted.

Meanwhile, the family which seems to be flourishing is the one in which the wife is chief earner and the husband stays at home and paints pictures of birds. Marge's job, which largely provides for them, is not in the world of business and profit, but in public service. Nor is it the kind of public service usually associated with women, teaching or nursing. It is a job more often associated with men. At the end of the film, this family has not lost members, but is about to gain a new one. It is intact, mutually supportive, content and growing. It is not a patriarchal, capitalist family, but is represented as a very normal, comfortable one.

cultural context

When studying any text, it is necessary to take into consideration its relationship to other contemporary cultural artefacts and dominant cultural ideas.

POSTMODERNISM AND POST-STRUCTURALISM

Most discussions of Coen works, including *Joel and Ethan Coen* (edited by Peter Korte and Georg Seesslen), will mention the term postmodern. This term has been used since the late Sixties, but refers particularly to the Eighties and Nineties. It is a complex concept for which there is no simple definition, but is characterised by a certain cynicism towards belief in modern progress, a doubting of the value of the supremacy of science and a questioning of the belief that the western world is the first, supreme world. In the postmodern age, high culture has been challenged by popular culture and there has been a blurring of the margins between the two. There may be a pessimism arising from the fact that it seems that no system (of government, of theory, of criticism, of art) works perfectly, therefore anything goes. Try anything because nothing works anyway. It is therefore not hard to see why the term postmodern is applicable for those who see the Coens' work as a heartless, cynical manipulation of style, done just for a laugh.

Others prefer to refer to post-structuralism. This term does not have the cynical nor the pessimistic connotations which the term postmodern has (though the two are inevitably connected). Like postmodernism, it refers to a pluralistic approach to art, government, theory or criticism, but without

cultural context

the belief that nothing works anyway. On the contrary, with the belief that there is something new to be discovered in the pluralistic approach. Hence, more meaning can be derived from Fargo by adopting a number of approaches, rather than by looking at it from a single perspective such as simply studying its director or its genre. It is more fruitful to explore the text, its director, its relationship with other texts and its relationship with audiences than simply to look at the text alone. Coen films hark back to films of another era, but adopt a new style in doing so which forces audiences to make comparisons and contrasts in order to extract all meanings and, one hopes, to understand something new, not *just* for a laugh, since why we laugh itself has significance. We would not think that Marge was such a funny detective, nor Jerry such a comic criminal, if we did not compare them with the ones with which we are more familiar. If we are laughing only at the quaint local accent, this could be deemed offensive. If we laugh because of the incongruity of that accent in a crime film, perhaps we are then noticing something about the nature of crime film itself. Post-structurally, a film is seen in the context of:

■ its relationship with other films (intertextuality). *Fargo* can be seen to be a deconstruction or exposé of the constructs of some previous crime films. The fact that the Coens seem to have made a film blanc might make us see film noir anew and very much as *a* style of crime film, not *the* style for crime film

■ the whole of the social, political and industrial system which produced it (director, writer, actors, producers, industrial relations, everything involved in the institution). The fact that the Coens chose to work independently of the mainstream, and with the team they choose, has meaning. They choose their team on the basis that those people will best help them to make the film they want to make. Often the previous work of personnel brings some meaning with it, e.g. Buscemi's lunatic image

■ the relationship between film and spectator/consumer/reader, i.e. audience, which may vary with individual reader/member of an audience, producing multiple meanings. Post-structurally, the ways in which a film makes meaning are seen as many, a far cry from seeing the film's director as the only source of meaning. Authors of meaning (those who endow a film with meaning) include writers, directors, genres, other films/ cultural works, stars, systems and audiences.

INTERTEXTUALITY

The first and most obvious reference to another text made by *Fargo* is in the title. In fact there are several films which contain the word 'Fargo' in their titles and they are largely Westerns. A film called *Wild Seed* (Brian Hutton, 1964) was also known as *Fargo* and was a romance, but otherwise, the name of this North Dakota town in a film title invariably signals a Western. Probably the best known is *Wells Fargo* (Frank Lloyd, 1937), the story of the express delivery service, an epic Western, later also to be used as the title of a television series based loosely on the film. Other Westerns with Fargo in their titles include *Fargo Express* (1933), *The Fargo Kid* (1941), *Fighting Bill Fargo* (1941), *Wells Fargo Gunmaster* (1951) and *Fargo* (1952). Audiences may well have expected, therefore, a Coen brothers' take on this genre, that is a film with big blue skies, big hats and horses, goodies and baddies, sheriffs and shoot-outs, saloon bar fights and a barber's shop, or at least an update of some of these. But, if only on the face of it, the Coens' *Fargo* is a cop story, a thriller, or at least a chiller. It has only one scene in Fargo, thereafter that town has no further relevance. This may be simply another Coen joke but if it is, then its punch line is not as simple as a 'Fooled you!' cry, for *Fargo* does have several Western characteristics (see Genre: *Fargo* the Western). The name *Fargo* simply sets in motion expectations, as does the caption about *Fargo*'s real life basis, which causes puzzlement and initiates debate.

Reference to TV programmes Although there is no direct reference to it by name in the script, there is little doubt that *Fargo* is making reference to a made-on-video comedy horror film of 1988, called *Woodchipper Massacre* (see Contexts: Filmography). This suggests that the most gruesome of all *Fargo*'s murders might have been based on a previously used idea and possibly that there might be some attempt to attract the attention of a similar audience.

There are allusions to television texts. *The Tonight Show Starring Johnny Carson*, watched by Gaear, Carl and the two hookers at the Blue Ox Motel is used perhaps because it is so familiar to Americans that they would know what time of day it was by knowing this was on television. They would also recognise it as an easy viewing piece of entertainment. The show has meaning for American audiences and is famous enough to be known by others too. Likewise, the episode of the soap which Gaear is watching as Carl returns with his jaw shot away (possibly an episode of a soap called *Generations*) signifies his involvement with the melodramatic scene on screen which in turn highlights his complete disregard for the woman he has recently killed lying behind him. It could possibly also be another time clue. Popular culture instantly has meaning for many people. It is something shared by many if not the majority and can be a short cut to revealing mood, time of day or night, taste and age. Marge and Norm watch a wildlife documentary just a touch more worthy than the viewing preferences of the killers.

Lack of reference to news stories The allusion to *Fargo* being a true story suggests that there ought to be texts somewhere which would bear this out, newspaper or television news stories for instance, but there probably are none. The introduction by Ethan Coen to the screenplay of *Fargo* tells of a story his Grandma used to tell to Joel and Ethan. She claimed it was true and they believed her for a long time. When older, they began to question the feasibility of Grandma's story and became sceptical. That made them question other stories she had told them, but there was never any evidence to the contrary. We might well question Marge's ability to assess a situation absolutely correctly first time.

We might wonder how she ever got the cuffs on Gaear. We might well wonder, having had the true life origin of the story of *Fargo* proclaimed to us, exactly how she did this. But there is no evidence to the contrary! As Ethan Coen suggests, perhaps we should take his story, as he did his grandmother's, at some sort of sceptical face value. In other words, claiming a basis in fact is a well-known storyteller's ploy.

filmography

The most obvious context of *Fargo* is within the body of Coen works. Each of the films by the Coen brothers relates in some way to *Fargo*. Each is both like and unlike all the others.

filmography

reality at a remove

Blood Simple (1984) is a thriller, that is a story of intrigue, infidelity and murder. It has some things in common with a film noir: seedy bars, motels, night scenes and a private detective starting off the narrative in voice-over. But it overturns our expectations of the noir thriller by using a Texas setting and by bringing in some genre stereotypes (e.g. the detective already mentioned) and then dashing those expectations (e.g. by having him played by a Western actor, M. Emmet Walsh, and also by having him turn out to be the murderer). Frances McDormand plays the leading female role as the wife trying to escape a husband she hates. (This film featured effects successfully taken up ten years later by Danny Boyle in *Shallow Grave* in Britain).

Raising Arizona (1987) is the first Coen kidnapping story in which a couple comprising an ex-convict and a policewoman steal a baby, and it is a comedy. In the way that a cartoon can allow dreadful things to happen for fun, so does *Raising Arizona* place reality at a remove so that we can laugh at very unfunny events. Frances McDormand plays a secondary role.

Miller's Crossing (1989) is gangster story containing as many details, twists and turns as *Blood Simple* if not more, before it tells us who did what. This film does not employ quite so broad a humour as the previous film, though there are wry moments and there is irony and some stereotypes used exaggeratedly for fun. It makes subtle points, one of which could be said to be a favourite Coen theme: that nobody really knows what anyone else is doing, let alone thinking or feeling. And in the case of *Miller's Crossing* it is the character who recognises and exploits this who survives, albeit alone. Coldness, secrecy and questions as to where honour and respect lie are recurring Coen themes. Irony (surprise caused by being led to think one thing then presented with another) is one of the weapons in their armoury.

Barton Fink (1991) is satire about Hollywood's so-called 'golden age'. In 1941, Barton Fink, a writer, having had Broadway success, is contracted to write for Hollywood. He then begins to suffer writer's block. A guest at the seedy hotel where Fink stays becomes his friend but turns out to be a violent, psychopathic killer. The film becomes not only a satire on Hollywood, but also a dark, gothic horror story, with blood and super-natural fires adding to Fink's problems. Its surrealism contrasts well with the realism in *Fargo*.

filmography

The Hudsucker Proxy (1994) is the Coen film which has received least critical acclaim. It is a pastiche of Hollywood comedies of the Forties, particularly those of Frank Capra which made a hero of the ordinary American man. This style, known as cornball or screwball comedy, tended to mythologise and sentimentalise the common man, whereas *Fargo* makes heroes of common folk, but sees them as comfortable and unassuming, not sentimental myths. In *The Hudsucker Proxy*, the life of an earnest business student nobody, Norville Barnes, has been exploited by manipulative, greedy vice-president Sydney Mussberger, to the point where Norville wants to end it all by jumping from a high building. He is saved from his fall by another lowly character, who jams a clock's mechanism thus stopping time, and he returns to work to succeed with the second of his simplistic ideas, the Frisbee (his first having been the hula-hoop: 'Y'know, for kids!').

Fargo, coming straight after the Coen film least liked by the critics, is probably the most liked to date. It is generally considered to contain the warmest representation of humanity. The film is, judged on its content, a thriller. But judged on its style, it does not seem that its first purpose is to thrill. It is witty and it is a comedy, but it is nevertheless a murder story. The murders are sparked off by a kidnapping and this is the second kidnap film from the Coens. But we must not forget that this one claims to be a true story. Is there a documentary element? Or have the Coens used that ploy simply to release them from the demands made by fictional narrative conventions, that everything should connect with the plot and that nothing should be redundant or unexplained? Some Western conventions are also used in *Fargo* (see Contexts: Genre).

The Big Lebowski (1998), the latest film from the Coen brothers, is yet another kidnap story and a thriller. Again the crime is bungled (by mistaken identity) and again there is macabre humour, much broader than in *Fargo*. Again, too, the genre aspect is not straightforward, for there is another seasoning of Western in the soup, and another ordinary guy comes out on top.

As well as seeing *Fargo* in the context of other Coen films, it might be appropriate to look at one or two other films which might relate to it in some way.

Woodchipper Massacre (1988), directed by Jon McBride, was a shot-on-video comedy horror movie which it seems likely that the Coens had come across and made reference to in *Fargo*. It had the tongue twisting tagline, 'How much flesh would a woodchipper chip if a woodchipper would chip flesh?' This matches the Coen macabre sense of humour and could have appealed to them.

High Sierra (1941) is a Raoul Walsh crime story starring Humphrey Bogart which has a snowy, countryside setting. It could be said, for several reasons, to be a film noir, but is unusual in that its anti-hero ends up dead in the snowy mountains after hiding out in a rustic cabin, rather than dead in a dark, neon-lit city street.

genre

Since the genre of *Fargo* as crime film is called into question as previously mentioned by the film's title – which suggests a Western – and its status as a true story is very shakey, we should perhaps examine its pedigree.

'Genre' is a term which means style, or kind, or category. Much American film falls into one or other of a number of genres: Western, gangster, thriller, gothic horror, science fiction, romance, melodrama, musical. Films tend to be categorised if they have enough of the characteristics or conventions of a genre to mark them out as belonging to it. In a sense a genre is like a family tree. From one original (the classic) spring many, like offspring. Each will be enough like the parent/classic to be labelled with the family/genre name, but will also be an individual with some characteristics of its own. Genres go through generations as do families. Marriages between genres e.g. gangster and Western give rise to new strains. Social and political conditions affect the generations, so that there is constant organic change, with the occasional throwback to the original or classic. As with many families, we could look at all the members and see that one is old and one is young, one is male and one is female, one is fair and one is dark etc. We may also be able to see that they are all members of the same family, because they all have some of the family characteristics: the nose, the eyes, the hair or teeth. So with genre films, they will all be conventional up to a point and individual and infinitely variable, too. The study of genre is the study of the mix of conventional and individual aspects of films. The possibilities for variation are inexhaustible. To look into genre is not to attempt to fit all film into a pre-formed mould of conventional proportions but provides a framework for looking at a popular film and its relation to other films. *Fargo*, it could be argued, has very mixed parentage!

FARGO THE WESTERN

Stefan Reinecke's chapter on *Fargo* in *Joel and Ethan Coen* (Peter Korte and Georg Seesslen (eds), pp. 186–187), refers to the film as 'post-Western' and as a 'feminist Western'. *Fargo* does have a bright, daytime look and a sense of wide open space. Country music plays in the bar in the first action scene. There is a rural setting for many scenes, and the city, Minneapolis, when used as a setting, is not seen as the big, dark claustrophobic place associated with many thrillers. Wade Gustafson is a stereotypical pioneer character, confident, self-righteous, never self-doubting. The bad guys are strangers in town, and the crime is cleaned up for the homely folk by a cop who has much in common with some slow-spoken sheriffs of the west. The pace is possibly more like that of a Western than a thriller and there are no fast car chases, but there is a native American Indian. Stefan Reinecke suggests that the expanses of snow signify wilderness, untamed territory. Marge, he says, 'combines the civilising mission of these women [teachers in westerns] with that outstanding virtue of the male westerner – the ability to do a job well and not to waste many words' (p. 187). Reinecke sees the men as foolish, violent, stumbling and lacking in insight, 'without which life in Coen films is guaranteed to be a failure.'

FARGO THE TRUE STORY

The words on the caption at the beginning of the film tell us we are going to see a true story. In keeping with the genre of films based on true stories are the film's camera style (see Style: Signifiers of the Real), the local Minnesota accent, the over-all apparent realism and the fact that some incidents do not connect with the plot whereas all events in a fiction usually do. Jerry's attempt to sell the car with TruCoat underseal and Marge's meeting with Mike Yanagita have no payoff, that is they are not in the chain of cause and effect with any plot or subplot, but probably function to show aspects of character (see Narrative and Form). Such examples of episodic structure are usually associated with true stories, biographies or documentary reconstructions. The police work has been de-dramatised, is seen as plodding, routine, careful and low-key. There is no action-packed heroism on the part of the cops, only good police work.

FARGO THE THRILLER

The seven murders and the detective work in *Fargo* ensure that it has to be seen as a thriller at least of some sort. Most reviews refer to it as a thriller, possibly because audiences expect some kind of genre label on films, to let them know what to expect. It would not be misleading to call it a thriller. Because we do not know on first viewing how many crimes will be committed and when, and we do not know whether the killers will be apprehended and how, this is a thriller. It is not a whodunnit mystery, but it is a how-will-they-catch'em movie. It is not exceptional in this. *Bonnie and Clyde* (Arthur Penn, 1967) had eponymous anti-heroes who led the authorities quite a dance until they were finally caught. The television detective series *Columbo* always lets the audience see the crime and the criminal, before watching as the detective uncovers the story for himself in much the same low-key but shrewd way as Marge does. In *Fargo* the main emphasis is not detection nor is it really on the crimes. The main point of the film is to make entertainment, but that entertainment does not arise from tour de force police work, nor from the terrifying crimes, nor from the engaged battle between almost equal forces of good and evil as might be conventional in a thriller. The main source of entertainment lies in the idiosyncratic way the story is told, in its comic style (see Style: Signifiers of Comedy). It ain't what it says, it's the way that it says it!

A COMEDY WESTERN THRILLER?

According to Joel Coen, as quoted by Stefan Reinecke (in Korte and Seesslen (eds), p. 170), '*Fargo* doesn't fit into any genre, so we had to warn the public in the opening credits.' He is referring to the 'True Story' caption at the start of the film.

Coen films are not spoofs, that is they are not quite comedies masquerading as one of the genres, because the point of them is not quite to make fun of the fact that classic genres were very conventional. There is something more complex than exaggerated impersonation of genre going on, but pastiche and playing with notions of genre are parts of it. Rather than exaggerate the stereotypes and conventions of the thriller as would a spoof, *Fargo* opposes some of them and uses some from other genres. Perhaps Coen movies are a genre in themselves, with their own set of conventions. Certainly it is not easy to discuss *Fargo* in terms of its similarity to other films, because it is both like and very unlike other genre films. As we have seen, it is only really like other Coen films, and even then, it is quite deliberately unlike them too.

production history

On Monday 30 August 1999, *Fargo* was the *Radio Times* film of the week, and the best part of a page was devoted to it. It was given a five star (top) rating and was said to be 'a deliciously twisted modern movie masterpiece'. Yet *Fargo* was exhibited on Channel Four, a channel whose remit was to cater for significant minorities. This indicates quite rightly, that this film is not a blockbuster, nor was it ever conceived as having mass appeal. And yet it did very well at box office in America, and in Europe. According to information on the Internet Movie Database, the budget for *Fargo* was seven million American dollars. It was released in the USA in March 1996 and one year later had grossed over twenty-four million dollars, most of that being made in the first four months. In Britain the film was released at the end of May 1996 and by July that year had taken over a million pounds. In France, admissions in September and October 1996 were over half a million and in Germany, where it was released in November, admissions were nearing 180,000 by December. *Fargo* was released in a further nineteen countries.

Such distribution cannot be seen as anything but wide, and behind it is the history of Coen brothers' movies, without which it would not have had the same distribution. Their first film, *Blood Simple* (1983) was made for $1.5 million, which took them eight months to raise. Their own parents were amongst contributors. They first made a three-minute trailer to show to prospective backers. The film took four years to make and the brothers had to work at other jobs whilst making it. It was successful at the New York and Toronto festivals and *Time* magazine listed it in its top ten films in 1985. After *Raising Arizona* and *Miller's Crossing*, the Coens gained recognition in Europe, but their biggest European success was *Barton Fink* which, at Cannes in 1991, won the Palme d'Or, John Turturro won best actor and Joel Coen best director.

Now, with a history of good box office receipts and critical acclaim, with a production company like Working Title, and all key personnel with previous successes, it is possible to understand why *Fargo* gained full support from the huge British-based PolyGram company (now, since May 1998, Universal Pictures International). PolyGram's USA distribution company, Gramercy Pictures (co-founded with Universal Studios), distributed *Fargo* in America.

The film sits at the point where art film meets the popular and is considered to be good commercial, but not blockbuster material. It is entertainment, but it is entertainment the way the Coens want to do it, not some kind of material made in response to the demands of focus groups. This artistic control is retained by the fact that the brothers write, produce, direct and edit their own work. Once they have secured a budget, they have a great deal of control over how it is spent. They have a group of people with whom they work repeatedly. e.g. some actors, Carter Burwell (Music), Roger Deakins (Director of Photography) and the production companies, Circle Films (the first four films) and Working Title Films, (their next three, up to *The Big Lebowski*). Working Title Films had produced *Four Weddings and a Funeral*, which commercially had been a hugely successful British film.

The role of Marge Gunderson was written with Frances McDormand (Mrs Joel Coen) in mind, that of Gaear for Peter Stormare and that of Carl for Steve Buscemi. Many think that McDormand and Buscemi (along with John Turturro and John Goodman) are at their best in Coen movies. There can be little doubt that there must have been considerable faith in the viability of the package being offered to backers in the film *Fargo*. The Coens began writing *Fargo* immediately after completing *The Hudsucker Proxy*. Since the

production history

executive producers, Tim Bevan and Eric Fellner at Working Title Films agreed to work with them again and to back them, the process of setting up the film was quite quick in film making terms, taking less than two years from first draft to the beginning of production.

Having secured their funding, the Coen brothers set about making their films in a carefully considered way. There have been many published articles and interviews with the brothers, e.g. *Hell Freezes Over* in *Sight and Sound* (May 1996, pp. 24–27), which includes three storyboard frames from the scene in which Gaear swings the axe at Carl. Such interviews often show something of their offhandedness in talking about their methods and intentions, but also show that they have a very definite and carefully planned vision of what they want. They work from details of each shot and camera movement, together with the screenplay.

For *Fargo* the original idea was to have only static shots, but this became tedious so Roger Deakins (regular collaborator, cinematographer and camera operator) used movement but kept it subtle, so that it did not intrude on the business of telling the story by drawing attention to itself.

The film was shot on location in Minneapolis, Minnesota, ironically in a mild winter, so that artificial snow had to be used. At the end of shooting, the outdoor scenes were shot and this was done in Dakota, in real snow.

The Coens' collaborators are good collaborators, and take direction. They are not in any sense auteurs themselves, but trust in the vision of the director. Having worked together before helps to build up a rapport and understanding of what is required to realise the vision. Having said that, some of the cast – or their previous roles – might have inspired some of the creation of character.

The name 'Roderick Jaynes' which appears on the credits as editor is a pseudonym. The Coens edit their films themselves. The editing of *Fargo* took only twelve weeks or so, less than usual for a Coen film. This is probably because of the quieter, more classic style using fewer shots and longer takes when compared with the others. An editor is used only if the schedule demands that editing must be going on at the same time as the shooting.

industrial context

The Coen brothers are said to be independent film makers, but independent from what?

HISTORICAL BACKGROUND

There was a time when American film was dominated by the big studios. Many of these owned cinema chains as well as their production systems, and so controlled production, distribution and exhibition. This 'studio era' of vertical integration began before sound came to the movies at the end of the Twenties, but the coming of sound forced the big studios to review their personnel, and gave them the opportunity to strengthen their position as employers. New talent was sought and signed up. The studios ensured that all newcomers were signed up long term and on contracts which favoured the studios, but gave security to staff, including actors. Under this system, throughout the Thirties and Forties and often well into the Fifties, Hollywood studios trained their own staff in their ways, hundreds of popular genre films were made in a modest, effective 'classical' narrative style and the American cinema industry in Hollywood thrived, becoming what most people in the English-speaking world thought of when they thought of film.

Three main forces caused this strong system to crumble:

■ Personnel became reluctant to sign further long-term contracts

■ The American Supreme Court ruled that the studios had too much power and must give up their cinema chains

■ Television entered the majority of homes and took away the audience

The old system crumbled, but movies continued to be made by an increasing number of independent companies.

INDEPENDENT PRODUCTION

The making of movies gradually underwent a change, so that by the Sixties, a more independent system had arrived in which people were on contract for the making of one film at a time. It was less restricting for them (e.g. actors could now direct, or produce, if they wished), but it was also much

industrial context

more risky. Once the big studios stopped training their staff, would-be film makers had to go elsewhere for training. One way of getting a grounding for prospective directors, was to attend a film school, sometimes attached to a university, and this is exactly what Joel Coen did, gaining an insight into film not only of Hollywood, but also of other countries and cultures. Robert Redford's Sundance organisation exists to encourage new talent, and has a festival for the screening of independent film. The many independent set-ups are reflected now in the many different movie styles. The Coens have experimented with style and in *Fargo*, returned to a somewhat more classical narrative (see Narrative and Form: Classical Narrative & Style).

New, independent production companies sprang up, but it was still the big studio businesses who handled distribution. There are, of course, shades of independence. If a company is prepared to work on a very small budget, to try to find distribution for itself, e.g in Film Societies and Film Festivals (of which there are hundreds), and in some specialist art-house independent cinemas which do not belong to chains, then that company can be truly its own boss, make any kind of film it wants, no matter how alternative to the mainstream, even though it may reach only a tiny audience. *Blood Simple* was made this way.

On the other hand, if a big distributor has become involved with the project, has even invested money, then that distributor can call at least some of the shots, e.g. it can insist that the project uses a certain production company or star, a certain composer etc. It is here, in this area of film production, that we find the Coens. An established production company, Working Title Films (*Four Weddings and a Funeral, Dead Man Walking,* as well as two other Coen films), and a very big distributor, PolyGram, took on the project of making and distributing *Fargo*. However, by writing their own films and insisting always that Ethan be producer (setting up schedules and deciding how the budget should be spent), Joel the director (with artistic control) and that the two of them should edit, the Coens manage to retain a great deal of control over their films. Since they have had successes, they are also in a position to influence decisions about the people with whom they work. Their first film, *Blood Simple*, was made as a truly independent venture and was successful because of success in festivals and popularity with film critics in the press. Since then, the brothers have contrived to have more mainstream distribution yet to hold onto their ethos and identity as 'indie' film makers.

Today's industries are often networked internationally. PolyGram Filmed Entertainment was a British-based company. Its distribution company in the USA, Gramercy, was co-founded with Universal Studios. In turn, PolyGram was a division of an international music and entertainment group. In May 1998, it was bought by Canadian owned Seagram (which also owns MCA/Universal Studios, thereby music, film and television) and called Universal Pictures International.

It is not easy to hold onto independence. Perhaps the Coens have found a niche on the borderline which suits them and their audiences well and perhaps they will contrive to stay there, independent but widely distributed.

audience

The study of audience includes:

■ Attempts to explain how film works on a spectator's mind, based on Freudian analysis. Film is seen as acting on our unconscious (male) desires (e.g. Metz, 1970s – see auteur/auteur theory in Hayward, 1996)

■ Feminist theory, critical of existing theory for seeing the relationship of film and viewer as a one-way thing (film acting on viewer), for seeing 'the viewer' as male, and for the assumption that there is a preferred or correct reading of a film (Laura Mulvey in Mulvey, 1989)

■ Further attempts (often from the feminist camp) to describe the relationship between film and audience, largely in terms of attempting to locate the focus of the pleasure to be found in film viewing (Mulvey and others in the 1980s)

■ Modern studies (often for television) which point to the fact that readings of film differ significantly with age, gender, nationality, sexuality and with class

Audiences are naturally very important and always have been to the industry. They have relatively recently become an area for study for film and media theorists. Work has been done on how audiences are positioned by a film, how they identify with the film and can be seen as active producers of meaning themselves. From being perceived as consumers, as passive spectators, then as readers and interpreters who decipher a film's messages, they are now seen by some as active makers of meaning by their own involvement in and relationship to the film. The nature of the society for whom films are made can, by its demands, be seen as producing the films it wants. Thus the relationship between film, film maker and audience can be seen as circular, all of them both receiving and sending out their own messages.

CONSTRUCTING AN AUDIENCE

Leonard Klady's review of *Fargo* in *Variety* (February 1996) says that the film will probably appeal to the same audience as *The Usual Suspects*, that is, a crossover of sophisticated and domestic commercial audiences.

Fargo was given an 18 Certificate in Britain, because of the violent content and so-called bad language. This is in not surprising since Coen films were never intended as family viewing. Although often insisting in interviews that their films are for fun and for kids, the Coens surely mean young adults rather than children. When Channel Four showed a series of Coen films, they used the line, 'Y'know, for kids', from *The Hudsucker Proxy* at the end of the montage introducing the series. It seems to encapsulate the intent to entertain the people who think as they do, see things as they do, i.e. their lack of intent to be seriously engaged in sending out didactic or philosophical messages. Their humour does, however, require a certain amount of intellectual engagement. It is not red-nosed humour for small children.

The poster advertising *Fargo* shows a cross-stitch sampler design, with a neat, homely border, around a dead body lying in the snow. The words 'a homespun murder story' appear under the cross-stitched title *Fargo*. A second (UK) poster, shows Carl in long shot in an expanse of snow, a fence disappearing into the distance, and a black bag right in the foreground. It is, of course the bag of ransom money. The poster has the slogan:

"A TERRIFIC TWISTED COMEDY A DAZZLING MIX OF MIRTH AND MALICE"

PETER TRAVERS · ROLLING STONE

A FILM BY JOEL AND ETHAN COEN

FARGO 18

SMALL TOWN
BIG CRIME
DEAD COLD

FRANCES   WILLIAM   STEVE
McDORMAND   H. MACY   BUSCEMI

POLYGRAM FILMED ENTERTAINMENT PRESENTS IN ASSOCIATION WITH WORKING TITLE FILMS 'FARGO' FRANCES McDORMAND WILLIAM H. MACY STEVE BUSCEMI HARVE PRESNELL PETER STORMARE MUSIC BY CARTER BURWELL PRODUCTION DESIGNER RICK HEINRICHS
DIRECTOR OF PHOTOGRAPHY ROGER A. DEAKINS, A.S.C. LINE PRODUCER JOHN CAMERON EXECUTIVE PRODUCERS TIM BEVAN ERIC FELLNER PRODUCED BY ETHAN COEN WRITTEN BY JOEL COEN AND ETHAN COEN DIRECTED BY JOEL COEN
ORIGINAL SCREENPLAY PUBLISHED BY FABER & FABER © ©1996 POLYGRAM FILM PRODUCTIONS B.V.

Film publicity poster used
in the UK: Carl in the snow
with the ransom money in the
foreground

A terrific twisted comedy
A dazzling mix of mirth and malice

and the film's title, large, blood red, is in the middle of the poster.

Taglines for this film include those already mentioned on the posters, and: 'A lot can happen in the middle of nowhere'; 'An ordinary place, an extraordinary thriller'; and possibly best of all, 'Small town. Big crime. Dead cold'. Those who find the posters and the taglines amusing, will probably find the film amusing, for the use of violence juxtaposed with humour is not only signalled, it is the very point of the jokes.

The distributors have an idea what kind of people might make up an audience for a film, based on research using several indicators:

■ The director's past popularity, with which groups

■ The popularity of the stars in the film, their 'fans'

■ The proven popularity of the film's genre with particular groups

They must target their publicity at the group they believe will make up the audience. Not since the collapse of the studio system have most films been made with family viewing in mind, and many films are now targeted at a group within the mass. It is the distributors' job to try to assess the composition of the target group, and to appeal to them, making best possible use of their budget in doing so.

A profile of a typical viewer and his/her lifestyle may be put together in an effort to best reach the audience with advertisements and information. However, even experienced distributors can fail. Audiences can be very elusive. Sometimes a film may not be perceived by the distributors as appealing to cinema goers, but rather to television viewers. It will have little cinema release and go quickly into video shops and onto movie channels. *Fargo* did not have blanket release, but was shown in selected cinemas.

Once a film has been marketed, word of mouth takes over and critical response becomes important.

critical responses

Critical responses to films can come in many forms. Television and the press have their film critics whose styles vary according to the audience or readership of the programme, newspaper or magazine. Some critics are well-known personalities themselves and may work in several media, appearing on television, writing regular columns in the press and publishing books. There are critics for young audiences who want entertainment and critics for audiences who want serious cultural discussion and every group in between. Film columns help sell magazines and vice versa. The function of such journalist-critics is to give an opinion or review of a new film and a review writer can be both entertaining for an audience and very necessary for the box office success of a film. Some critics delve a little deeper and go into an analysis of a film, possibly in the context of other films at the time, or other films from the same director or star. They may give opinions about the place of the film in our culture, relate it to current social issues etc. They may work in late night cultural programmes, or on talk radio, or the more serious or specialist magazines. Still more extensive discussion is provided by the writers of books, who may write a whole book on a particular genre or director. Some books are compiled of essays on serious and searching topics related to film and it is here that we might find film theorists examining film and ideology, or film and meaning, the more abstract issues related to film. *Fargo* has been the subject of examples of all these branches of film criticism (reviews, critical analyses and theory).

BOOKS

Contemporary Hollywood Cinema by Steve Neale and Murray Smith (eds) is a collection of individual essays on many aspects of contemporary Hollywood, industry, philosophy, economy, aesthetics and technology. It contains an essay by Hilary Radner, called *New Hollywood's new women: murder in mind – Sarah and Margie*. This looks at the two main female roles in *Terminator 2: Judgment Day* and *Fargo*. Marge's image is analysed and interpreted in psychoanalytical terms from a feminist standpoint and said to refuse to be fetishised or made the object of cinematic scopophilia.

critical responses

Whilst Marge's body is very much present – vomiting, eating and being quite a load – it is not offered for voyeurs, defying Hollywood machinery.

Geoffrey Andrews's book *Stranger than Paradise: Maverick Film-makers in Recent American Cinema* is about directors, perhaps auteurs, who oppose the mainstream in some way and includes a chapter on the Coens, with David Lynch, Wayne Wang, Jim Jarmusch, Spike Lee and Quentin Tarantino being amongst the others. The chapter on the Coens deals briefly with each of their films up to and including *The Big Lebowski*. It identifies common themes (violence, deceit, distrust, not knowing what other people are doing) and common aspects of style (juxtaposition of comedy and horrific violence). *Fargo*, it says, shows a new maturity, a more classical visual style and a respectful depiction of mutually supportive marriage, warmth and simplicity (not sentimentality) and a delightful wit.

Joel and Ethan Coen by Peter Korte and Georg Seesslen (eds) looks at the Coens as auteurs and contains a chapter on each of their films up to 1998, each of which is a critical essay by a different author (Seesslen wrote two). The *Fargo* chapter is by Stefan Reinecke. It is illustrated by lots of frames from the film, and looks at fact/fiction and the narrative, violence as caused by male impotence and rage and violence as (almost) accident. It looks at the representation of the two families, the Lundegaards and the Gundersons, and sees *Fargo* as a descendant of the Western, with the women as civilising influences on unruly men.

PRESS REVIEWS

Reviews of *Fargo* appeared in many newspapers and magazines. The vast majority of the opinions expressed were favourable, with a minority expressing reservations (see also Background: Trailer).

The quieter camera and editing style of the film compared with previous Coen works was generally applauded as suitable for the subject and found positively beautiful by some writers e.g. William Leith in the *Mail on Sunday* (2 June 1996, p. 31), who found it 'a subtle, beautifully photographed thriller'. Philip French in the *Observer Review* (2 June 1996, p. 10) calls it 'an adroit piece of story-telling', and Geoff Brown in the *Times* (30 May 1996, p. 37) praises Joel Coen's 'masterful control over the images' and his encouragement of British cinematographer, Roger Deakins, to find 'eerie beauty even in a snow-capped parking lot, criss-crossed by shadows from the wintry sun'.

The press praised the quality of acting in *Fargo*, particularly that of Frances McDormand and William H. Macy. Macy is said by Christopher Tookey in the *Daily Mail* (31 May 1996, p. 36) to give 'a sensational performance, funny but also sad, as a weak but not intrinsically evil man, entangled in just such a waking nightmare'. Tookey also refers to Frances McDormand as 'one of the finest screen actresses in the US'. Will Cohu in the *Sunday Express* (2 June 1996, p. 59) picks out Macy for comment, as 'This pathetic wretch, brilliantly sketched by William Macy', and William Leith (see previous paragraph) also notes that 'The little car dealer is played by William H. Macy, whose small, crumpled face reflects our emotions throughout the film; we feel his guilt and his fear'. Frances McDormand's face is said to be 'benign, jowly, endlessly watchable' by Jonathon Coe in the *New Statesman* (7 June 1996, p. 36). Although the Oscar went to Frances McDormand, there is at least as much praise for Macy in the press, maybe more.

Many reviewers comment on the new warmth and maturity of *Fargo* in comparison with previous Coen movies, which are often said to be clever but cold. The respect for the values of ordinary folk was seen as something of a coming of age of Joel and Ethan Coen, and the underlying morality and decency were applauded, as was the depiction of a mutually supportive marriage. Jonathon Coe expresses appreciation of *Fargo*'s moral values when he says:

> Watching this taut, witty, expertly performed film, I found myself suspecting that the Coen Brothers, always a step or two ahead of their mainstream counterparts, had conceived it not just as an entertainment but as an intervention in the snowballing debate about screen violence. Certainly no other recent American thriller has attempted to put its carnage into such an explicitly moral context: the vigour with which all the bad guys are brought to justice would have satisfied the most stringent requirements of the Hays Office

> *Jonathon Coe in The New Statesman, 7 June 1996, p. 36*

critical responses

The humour in *Fargo* was almost universally enjoyed by reviewers. Alexander Walker in the *Evening Standard* (30 May 1996) refers to the Coens' 'askew view of the ordinary'. Christopher Tookey (see above) writes of 'a cool, very black comedy'. Anne Billson in the *Sunday Telegraph* (2 June 1996, p. 9) finds the film's criminals 'squirm-makingly funny'.

Quentin Curtis in the *Daily Telegraph* (31 May 1996, p. 22) tempers his admiration for the film with a little suspicion. He is not convinced that the Coens have found hearts and whilst he admires their humour, technical brilliance and the 'top-notch' quality of the acting, he still perceives a hollowness and a chill in the work. Georgia Brown in the *Village Voice* (12 March 1996) is more uncompromising in her distaste for this and other Coen work. She calls it 'another acrid blast of tail-wind', and writes of its 'dank slapstick', and dislikes nearly all the characters from the 'bug eyed dork of a husband' (Norm) to the 'chirpy nitwit' (Jean). Marge she damns with faint praise, finding her the only decent character. Ms Brown wishes that some of the Coens' 'hipster' fans would relieve her of the burden of writing about the film.

It seems, where reviews are concerned, you win some and you lose some.

bibliography

general film

Altman, Rick, *Film Genre,*
Routledge, 1981
Detailed exploration of film genres

Bordwell, David, *Narration in the Fiction Film,* Routledge, 1985
A detailed study of narrative theory and structures

– – – *The Classical Hollywood Cinema: Film Style & Mode of Production to 1960,* Routledge, 1985; pprbk 1995
An authoritative study of cinema as institution, it covers film style and production

Bordwell, David & Thompson, Kristin, *Film Art,* McGraw-Hill, 4th edn, 1993
An introduction to film aesthetics for the non-specialist

Branson, Gill & Stafford, Roy, *The Media Studies Handbook,* Routledge, 1996

Buckland, Warren, *Teach Yourself Film Studies,* Hodder & Stoughton, 1998
Very accessible, it gives an overview of key areas in film studies

Cook, Pam (ed.), *The Cinema Book,* British Film Institute, 1994

Corrigan, Tim, *A Short Guide To Writing About Film,* HarperCollins, 1994
What it says: a practical guide for students

Dyer, Richard, *Stars,* London BFI, 1979
A good introduction to the star system

Easthope, Antony, *Classical Film Theory,* Longman, 1993
A clear overview of recent writing about film theory

Hayward, Susan, *Key Concepts in Cinema Studies,* Routledge, 1996

Hill, & Gibson (eds), *The Oxford Guide to Film Studies,* Oxford, 1998
Wide-ranging standard guide

Lapsley, Robert & Westlake, Michael, *Film Theory: An Introduction,* Manchester University Press, 1994

Maltby, Richard & Craven, Ian, *Hollywood Cinema,* Blackwell, 1995
A comprehensive work on the Hollywood industry and its products

Nelmes, Jill (ed.), *Introduction to Film Studies,* Routledge, 1996
Deals with several national cinemas and key concepts in film study

Nowell-Smith, Geoffrey (ed.), *The Oxford History of World Cinema,* Oxford, 1996
Hugely detailed and wide-ranging with many features on 'stars'

Thomson, David, *A Biographical Dictionary of the Cinema,* Secker & Warburg, 1975
Unashamedly driven by personal taste, but often stimulating

Truffaut, François, *Hitchcock,* New York, Simon & Schuster, 1966, rev.ed. Touchstone, 1985
Landmark extended interview

Turner, Graham, *Film as Social Practice,* Routledge, 1993

Wollen, Peter, *Signs and Meaning in the Cinema,* New York, Viking 1972
An important study in semiology

Readers should also explore the many relevant websites and journals. *Film Education* and *Sight and Sound* are standard reading.

Valuable websites include:

The Internet Movie Database at
http://uk.imdb.com/

Screensite at
http://www.tcf.ua.edu/screensite/contents.htm

The Media and Communications Site at the University of Aberystwyth at
http://www.aber.ac.uk/~dgc/welcome.html

There are obviously many other university and studio websites which are worth exploring in relation to film studies.

fargo

British Film Institute,
Data copyright 1993–97,

Film Index International,
CD Rom,
Chadwyk-Healey Ltd, 1993–97

Andrew, Geoff, *Stranger than Paradise: Maverick Film-makers in Recent American Cinema,*
Prion Books Ltd, 1998
Contains a chapter on the Coen brothers with reference to each of their films

Coen, Ethan & Coen, Joel, *Fargo,*
Faber and Faber, 1996

Korte, Peter & Seesslen, Georg,
Joel and Ethan Coen,
Titan Books, 1999 (translated from

German by Rory Mulholland, published in German by Dieter Bertz Verlag, 1998)
Contains a chapter on each Coen film by a variety of writers, an interview with the Coens and an analysis of what makes a Coen film, *Looking for a Trail in Coen County*

Mulvey, Laura,
Visual and Other Pleasures,
Macmillan, 1985
A feminist approach

Neale, Steve & Smith, Murray, (eds),
Contemporary Hollywood Cinema,
Routledge, 1998
Contains a chapter on new roles for women in 'new' Hollywood, with reference to Frances McDormand's role of Marge Gunderson in *Fargo*

cinematic terms

auteur/authorship usually refers to a film director of particular acclaim or status, but in a wider sense can refer to anyone who originates meaning in a film, hence auteur theory, the debate about just who endows a film with meaning

bathos anticlimax, or deliberate drop from the intense to the ordinary for (usually) comic effect

black humour dark, gruesome, usually involving death; humorous treatment of a subject which is not itself funny at all

blanket release released to be shown in cinemas all over the country at the same time

causal link a link between two events in a story where one event has caused, or been caused by another

Cahiers group French film critics who opened the debate about who should be considered as auteur in the magazine *Cahiers du Cinema* during the Fifties

character actor an actor known for playing somewhat eccentric roles

close up a shot in which a particular subject fills most of the frame; if the subject is a person, a shot of head and shoulders, close to the camera, therefore large in the frame

closure the closing or rounding off of all the chains of events in a story; the point at which all the events linked by cause and effect come to an end; resolution of all enigmas, quests, and chains of action

continuity the illusion of continuous action achieved in film making by joining shots (which may have been done at a number of different times) together with great care, to match

everything up so that they look as if the action is continuous (see also eyeline match, match on action and shot/reverse-shot)

cornball a nickname for a person coming from the countryside or a rural background

counter cinema cinema which deliberately opposes mainstream cinema in some way, in either form or content, or both

dead time time in which nothing is going on that is connected with the story

deconstruction a process of revealing the codes and conventions of mainstream (i.e. popular) cinema

diegesis/diegetic the world and events of the film's story make up the diegesis (including things which have happened but not been shown, e.g. the birth of a baby may not be shown but may be part of the diegesis if it is presumed by the story to have happened). Mood music which the audience can hear but is not really meant to be taking place in the film's world is said to be non–diegetic

director the person in charge of everything that happens in front of the camera, who has last word on any artistic decisions, who directs the actors and who liaises with the design team for the shots she or he wants

distribution the task of promoting a film and getting it into cinemas, onto television, video etc. after it has been produced, because distributors hold the film's copyright

ellipses a missed out period of (usually) unimportant) time so that a story covering perhaps a year can be shown in

cinematic terms

a film of under two hours; sometimes marked by a fade

executive producer person in charge of the business aspect of making of a film, who raises the required money and is in charge of the hiring, employing and firing (if necessary) of personnel, remote from the hands-on production of the film

eye-line match an aspect of continuity editing; helping the shots to make sense across cuts and joins by ensuring that eyes in one shot are looking in the correct direction to match logically with what they are supposed to be looking at

fade out a shot which gradually darkens to a plain black screen, or lightens to a plain white; a fade in is a black or white screen which gradually changes to a shot

film noir a film about murder and crime with a particular dark expressionistic visual style achieved by low key lighting and no fill light, creating shadows and dark corners

genre type or classification of popular narrative film e.g. Western, horror, science fiction, melodrama

Hays Office the committee headed by Will Hays who put together the Production Code for the Hollywood studios, a form of self censorship during the Thirties and Forties

independent outside the mainstream, often alternative or counter to the mainstream

intertextuality the deliberate referring by one film text to another

juxtaposition placing or being placed side by side, or in the case of cinematic shots, one directly after another

long shot a shot in which the subject can be seen full length and in its surroundings, somewhat distanced from the camera

low-key lighting key lighting is the bright light which lights up the subject of a shot: low-key lighting keeps this low, usually uses no fill light and hence creates dark corners and high contrast between light and dark areas

match on action an aspect of continuity editing whereby two different shots of the same action are joined or 'cut' together at exactly the same point in the gesture or movement, giving the illusion of continuous action

medium shot a shot in which the subject is seen in moderate size; a person would be seen waist up, filling much of the screen

mise-en-scène the dividing of the film into shots which will tell the story, the staging and framing of those shots

payoff result; the reason why something has been drawn to our attention in a film

postmodern (of an age or era) the Eighties and Nineties; a style which can be used to describe a film, novel or other cultural artefact; it is characterised by a certain cynicism, a rejection of modernist optimism and a belief in progress via science, a rejection of belief that the western world is the best world; a pluralist approach to making meaning based on using, or referring to, any style from any age from any culture in order to say what needs saying

post-structuralism a pluralistic approach to film criticism; the idea that

cinematic terms

a single or total theory about how meaning is made in film is inadequate. Post-structuralist approaches examine all possible making of meaning revolving around a text and seem to say that the authors of meaning are within the text, its creator, its relationship with other texts and its audience

producer the person who organises the production of a film, allocates time and money to the necessary procedures, fixes schedules and makes sure everything is in the right place at the right time

production the actual making of all the parts of a film: preproduction is the planning and writing stage, production is the making, and post-production is the assembling of the parts

scopophilia the desire to see, especially that which gives pleasure

screwball a nickname for a person who is eccentric or just a little crazy, a likeable eccentric

shot/reverse shot a well-used way of showing a conversation, editing alternating shots of the couple conversing, each as if seen over the shoulder of the other with careful eyeline matches so that they seem to be looking at each other

structuralism a theory about how film makes sense to us which holds that there are underlying structures in human understanding common to all cultures, like language systems. A theory related to linguistics and semiotics

tagline a succinct, catchy line or phrase used in the promotion of a film, similar to a slogan

two shot a shot in which two people are framed equally, usually using a medium shot

vertical integration a type of industrial organisation where the production, distribution and sale or exhibition of a product are all owned by the same organisation, like the Hollywood Studio System

voice-over a non-diegetic voice which narrates a film or parts of it. This can be the voice of one of the characters, but there is nowhere in the diegesis where that character could realistically be saying those words, since they are addressed to the audience and not to anyone in the world of the film itself

credits

distributor
PolyGram (now UPI))

director
Joel Coen

producer
Ethan Coen

screenplay
Ethan Coen, Joel Coen

**director of
photography**
Roger Deakins

editor
Roderick Jaynes

art director
Thomas P. Wilkins

production designer
Rick Heinrichs

music
Carter Burwell

executive producers
Tim Bevan, Eric Fellner

head of production
Jane Frazer

line producer
John Cameron

**production
co-ordinator**
Karen Ruth Getchell

**unit production
manager**
Gilly Ruben

location manager
Robert J. Graf

**post-production
supervisor**
Margaret Hayes

assistant directors
Michelangelo Csaba Bolla
James Allen Hensz
Brian O'Kelley
Donald Murphy

script supervisor
T. Kukovinski

casting
John Lyons

location casting
Jane Brody

camera operator
Robin Brown

**special effects
co-ordinator**
Paul Murphy

credits

storyboard artist
J. Todd Anderson

graphic artist
Bradford Richardson

set director
Lauri Gaffin

costume designer
Mary Zophres

costume supervisor
Sister Daniels

key make-up artist
John Blake

titles designer
Balsmeyer & Everett

music editor
Todd Kassov

supervising sound editor
Skip Lievsay

opticals
John Alagna Effects House

dialogue editors
Magdaline Volaitis,
Frederick Rosenberg

adr editor
Kenton Jakub

foley editors
Bruce Pross, Frank Kern,
Stephen Visscher

foley mixer
Ezra Dweek

foley artist
Marko Constanzo

sound mixer
Allan Byer

music scoring mixer
Michael Farrow

re-recording mixers
Michael Barry, Skip Lievsay

sound effects editors
Eugene Gearty, Lewis Goldstein,
Glenfield Payne

stunt co-ordinator
Jery Hewitt

credits

cast

Marge Gunderson – Frances McDormand

Carl Showalter – Steve Buscemi

Gaear Grimsrud – Peter Stormare

Jerry Lundegaard – William H. Macy

Wade Gustafson – Harve Presnell

Jean Lundegaard – Kristin Rudrud

Scotty Lundegaard – Tony Denman

Irate Couple – Gary Houston & Sally Wingert

Car Salesman – Kurt Schweikhardt

Hookers – Larissa Kokernot & Melissa Peterman

Shep Proudfoot –Steven Reevis

Reilly Diefenbach – Warren Keith

Morning Show Hosts – Steve Edelman & Sharon Anderson

Stan Grossman – Larry Brandenburg

State Trooper – James Gaulke

Victim in Car – Michelle Suzanne Le Doux

Norm Gunderson – John Carroll Lynch

Lou – Bruce Bohne

Cashier – Petra Boden

Mike Yanagita – Steve Park

Customer – Wayne Evenson

Officer Olson – Cliff Rakerd

Hotel Clerk – Jessica Shepherd

Airport Lot Attendant – Peter Schmitz

Mechanic – Steve Schaeffer

Escort – Michelle Hutchinson

Man in Hallway – David Lomax

Himself – Jose Feliciano

Night Parking Attendant – Don William Skahill

Mr Mohra – Bain Boehlke

Valerie – Rose Stockton

Bismarck Cops – Robert Ozasky & John Randemer

Bark Beetle Narrator – Don Wescott

Source: *Sight and Sound*, Vol. 6, Issue 6, British Film Institute, pp. 40–41

Other titles in the series

Other titles available in the York Film Notes series:

Title	ISBN
8½	0582 40488 6
A Bout de Souffle	0582 43182 4
Apocalypse Now	0582 43183 2
Battleship Potemkin	0582 40490 8
Blade Runner	0582 43198 0
Casablanca	0582 43201 4
Chinatown	0582 43199 9
Citizen Kane	0582 40493 2
Das Cabinet des Dr Caligari	0582 40494 0
Double Indemnity	0582 43196 4
Dracula	0582 43197 2
Easy Rider	0582 43195 6
Fargo	0582 43193 X
La Haine	0582 43194 8
Lawrence of Arabia	0582 43192 1
Psycho	0582 43191 3
Pulp Fiction	0582 40510 6
Romeo and Juliet	0582 43189 1
Some Like It Hot	0582 40503 3
Stagecoach	0582 43187 5
Taxi Driver	0582 40506 8
Terminator	0582 43186 7
The Full Monty	0582 43181 6
The Godfather	0582 43188 3
The Piano	0582 43190 5
The Searchers	0582 40510 6
The Third Man	0582 40511 4
Thelma and Louise	0582 43184 0
Unforgiven	0582 43185 9

Also from York Notes

Also available in the **York Notes** range:

York Notes

The ultimate literature guides for GCSE students (or equivalent levels)

York Notes Advanced

Literature guides for A-level and undergraduate students (or equivalent levels)

York Personal Tutors

Personal Tutoring on essential GCSE English and Maths topics

Available from good bookshops.

For full details, please visit our website at www.longman-yorknotes.com

notes

FARGO